OLDSMOBILE
Muscle Cars

William Holder & Phillip Kunz

Motorbooks International
Publishers & Wholesalers ®

First published in 1994 by Motorbooks International Publishers & Wholesalers, PO Box 2, 729 Prospect Avenue, Osceola, WI 54020 USA

Motorbooks International books are also available at discounts in bulk quantity for industrial or sales-promotional use. For details write to Special Sales Manager at the Publisher's address

Library of Congress Cataloging-in-Publication Data Available

ISBN 0-87938-957-5

On the front cover: Olds muscle at both ends of the spectrum: Robert Lamons' 1969 Hurst/Olds, one of the premier Olds models, and Dennis Arnold's 1968 Cutlass Convertible, a high–performance muscle car in all but name. *Phillip Kunz*

On the frontispiece: The classy 1967 442. *Phillip Kunz*

On the title page: Two of father and son Bob and Charles Baxter's finest; a 1970 W-30 and a 1970 Rallye 350. *Phillip Kunz*

Printed and bound in the United States of America

Contents

Foreword

The Oldsmobile experience began for me in 1966 when I tagged along with my dad to a new car showroom. We stood in front of a shiny red Oldsmobile and I remember him saying, "The Olds 442, it's the hottest thing on the street." To this day, I remember staring at those neat-looking louvers on the hood.

In 1972, I was reading car magazines at the local drug store when I came across a headline that read "Factory Blueprinted Olds 442, the 455 W-30 package turns Olds dressed-up Cutlass S into an animal." I thought, something *more* than a 442? The lead photograph was a full-page head shot of a W-30 smoking the tires out of the hole! The seed that had been planted years before was now in full bloom. I was seventeen at the time, and on a mission.

Back then, Oldsmobile built cars to fulfill dreams. The "W" series brought the power, handling, and looks of the 442 to a new level, offering ultimate performance in either small- or big-block configurations.

Even today, few people realize the awesome potential of the lighter W-31, which is capable of putting out almost one horsepower per cubic inch. More people are aware of the enormous torque of the big-block W-30 cars, which stole the spotlight from the Pontiac GTO at the racetrack in 1966.

Olds established an arrangement with Hurst Performance in 1968, packaging a larger motor and more torque in a tasteful combination of looks and power. The W-32 offered performance between that of the 442 and the all-out W-30. In 1970, a Rallye 350 was introduced to offer the Olds performance image for those on a budget, and Indy pace cars joined the club, adding a beautiful dress-up package to the 442 or Cutlass.

In the sixties and seventies, Oldsmobile fulfilled dreams with looks, sounds, and sensational performance, the likes of which have not been seen since.

Three months after I read that article in 1972, my dad allowed me to finance my dream—a 1970 442 W-30. For this I am eternally grateful. I still own my 1970 W-30, and a short drive down the road always makes a bad day better.

—*Bill Streeter,*
National Oldsmobile Performance Enthusiast

Acknowledgments

All photos by Phillip Kunz
We want to thank the following people for their help in making this book possible:
Ed and Elizabeth Shaudys
Oldsmobile Club of America
Mike Furman
Oldsmobile Historical Archives
Harvey Freeman
Bill Streeter
Rick Blowers
Dennis Urban

Introduction

To many, the words "muscle car" and "Oldsmobile" go together like oil and water. Unlike Chevrolet and Pontiac, the name Oldsmobile has never connoted performance.

A recent advertisement for an Olds performance model was the final straw for vintage Oldsmobile lovers. The ad for the new model proclaimed, "It's not your father's Oldsmobile!" The underlying message here was that the sixties and seventies Olds machines didn't have what it took.

That ad writer probably wasn't even around when those models were new. Unfortunately, the writer was probably referring to the massive 88 and 98 boats of the era. But that wasn't all Olds represented—not even close!

An Oldsmobile performance image began building in the 1950s with the evolution of the Olds 88 powerplant. The car maker also introduced a tri-carb powerplant in the late fifties, an event that almost went unnoticed, and the manufacturer pioneered turbocharging in the early sixties.

The introduction of the sporty and spirited 442 in late 1964 was the first solid step into the muscle car performance world by the Oldsmobile Motor Division of General Motors Corporation. The 442, though, started out as nothing more than a performance option with a 330ci powerplant.

Prepped with a 400ci displacement mill in 1965, the reputation of the 442 continued to escalate, with the 442 growing from an option to a full-fledged model for 1968. The Olds muscle love affair dropped off in the early years of the decade.

Several other performance fall-outs took place during that awesome era. In the late sixties, the normally conservative Oldsmobile division came up with an exciting series of "W" cars which set the hot-rod market on its ear.

The W options consisted of the W-30, W-31, and W-32, which could be installed on several different models. There were also a number of variations that were not advertised. The W options included forced air induction, high-performance carburetors and cams, special handling and suspension systems, and more. Collectors consider these powerful and stylish W machines some of the most desirable muscle cars.

Then there were the magnificent Hurst/Olds machines, which were Olds 442s equipped with 455ci engines and modified by Hurst.

Oldsmobile earned yet another distinction during the muscle car era. It was selected four times as an Indy pace car, an honor that brought an unbelievable amount of publicity to the manufacturer.

A number of other A-body Olds machines could be ordered during this period that qualify as muscle cars. Collectors find these plain-Jane models with muscular powerplants (assuming they're factory pieces) especially appealing.

There are also some miscellaneous muscle-era cars worthy of note. First, there was the single-year model, the 1970 Rallye 350, a bright yellow bird that really caught your eye. For several years, the SX model could, with a little innovative ordering in the showroom, be quite a muscle car.

Totally unnoticed at the time was the array of non-W, non-442 Cutlass models, whose stock powerplants provided significant performance. The fact that these models could produce well over 300hp is often forgotten.

Like many car manufacturers, Oldsmobile performance languished at low levels during the early eighties, but started to return during the latter part of the decade. The big-bore performance of the four-cylinder Quad 4 mill indicated the company's commitment to high performance.

In the early nineties, horsepower edged back toward that magical three hundred level. As of this writing, Oldsmobile has started to move back into the forefront of modern performance with its new Aurora model.

In spite of the car maker's continued progress in reclaiming its high-performance image, Oldsmobile discontinued factory participation in National Association for Stock Car Automobile Racing (NASCAR) stock car racing, after an illustrious history in the sport. However, Oldsmobiles continue to run competitively in the National Hot Rod Association (NHRA) drag racing arena where they have done well in the Pro Stock class.

With that brief history of Oldsmobile performance in mind, let's examine the well-known and the not-so-well-known Olds muscle cars from the forties through the nineties. It's quite a story!

"88"

Make a Date with a "Rocket 8"!

A General Motors Value

OLDSMOBILE

Oldsmobile Hydra-Matic Drive, at reduced price, optional on all models. Series "88" and "98" models powered by "Rocket" Engine.

Chapter 1

Early Olds Performance

Most recall the famed Oldsmobile's of the late sixties and early seventies; the awesome 442, the W modifications, and the Hurst creations. But younger performance enthusiasts might not realize that the Olds muscle image was born much earlier. The Olds performance heritage goes as far back as the fifties, when the famous Rocket 88-powered machines performed magnificently in the early NASCAR days. During those early years, the GM division was at the forefront in high-performance technology. The development of the Rocket powerplant and a fairly light platform made the 88 one of the first muscle cars.

The 1949 Rocket engine was an industry-leading performer produced during a period when Olds brass were looking more toward economy. But that magnificent mill was attracting unexpected publicity with its success in NASCAR racing.

Oldsmobile 88s won six of the eight NASCAR races in 1949 and Olds driver Red Byron became the Grand National champion. Joe Littlejohn and his 88 coupe averaged 100.28mph at Daytona Speed Week, smashing a record set fourteen years earlier. Hershel McGriff and Ray Elliott won the 1949 Carrera Panamericana road race in an Oldsmobile. The fact that an Olds 88 convertible paced the Indy 500 that year didn't hurt Oldsmobile's performance image either.

Oldsmobile domination continued the following year, despite the fact that a standard transmission was not available on the stock 88. Even with an automatic, the 88 won ten of nineteen NASCAR races. The wins went to Curtis Turner (with four) and Dick Linder (with three). Single victories went to Fonty Flock, Fire-ball Roberts, and Grand National Champion Bill Rexford.

The vaunted 88 powerplant showed its stuff on the international scene as well, winning the 2,100 mile Carrera Panamericana that year and the French Apa-Francor-champs for two straight years. The 88 mill was definitely the powerplant to beat, with lots of great advertising to go along with it. The performance image apparently caught the buying public's attention since well over four hundred thousand bought Oldsmobiles, with about 65 percent of the

Early Rocket powerplants were real killers, with maintenance-free hydraulic lifters, aluminum pistons, forged crank, and full-floating wrist pins. This particular Rocket is of 1950 vintage.

This early ad touts the Oldsmobile Rocket 88, an engine that brought the company considerable success in early NASCAR racing. **Oldsmobile advertisement**

No doubt about the Rocket heritage of this 1955 hummer. Horsepower ratings were on the rise with 202 ponies available in 1955 and 1956.

This famous rocket symbol was the sign of Olds performance in the forties and fifties. This example adorns the sheet metal of a 1950 Olds 88.

buyers choosing the 88 powerplant.

The fabulous Flock brothers burned up the NASCAR tracks in 1951 with fourteen wins between them. Turner came home with a pair of wins. In all, Olds 88 machines took almost half the victories, winning twenty out of forty-one races. Olds domination on the tracks, though, came to an end in the early 1950s with the introduction of the low-slung dual-carb Hudson Hornet. No longer able to sustain

the successes of the glory years, Oldsmobile withdrew from NASCAR competition in the mid-sixties.

During the glory days, the Olds 88 was the superstar of the series, the performance machine of many of the front runners. It must be remembered that NASCAR race cars of that era were nearly stock with few changes made to factory specs. It was a time distinctly different from today, when the only thing stock about the custom-built NASCAR race machines is the shape of the sheet metal.

The early Rocket 88 powerplant incorporated a number of significant features; an overhead valve-train with quiet, maintenance-free hydraulic lifters, an oversquare bore-stroke ratio, a forged crank with six counterweights, aluminum pistons, full-floating wrist-pins, and a dual-plane intake manifold.

But, by today's standards, the horsepower figures of those early machines were anemic at best. The 88 mills of 1949 displaced 303.7ci, but produced only 135hp, a top power rating for the time. Even so, the 88 accelerated from zero-to-sixty mph in twelve seconds.

In NASCAR, Oldsmobiles won ten out of nineteen Grand National events in 1951, twenty out of

They didn't call these machines "muscle cars" back in the fifties, but they certainly qualified as such. This classy-looking 1956 Rocket powerplant was capable of pumping out more than 200hp.

forty-one races in 1951, and the championship both years. Without doubt, the Oldsmobile was the car to beat during the 1950s. The horsepower remained at the 135 level through the 1951 model year. In 1952, the power was kicked up in a big way to 160 horses.

After the popularity of the initial Rocket mills, Olds saw the light and continued to increase the output of the powerplant. In 1954, two versions of the powerplant were produced with 170hp and 185hp. Engine tweaks included nudging the compression ratio up to 8.25:1, with a healthy four-barrel carburetor replacing the two-barrel of the earlier Rockets. The impressive performance was accomplished with six less cubic inches.

Performance continued at a high level in 1955 with the same 185 horses and 320lb-ft of torque, perking at an 8.5:1 compression ratio. It should be noted that cam and piston problems caused these models to spend some time in the garage.

With the aid of a 9.25:1 compression ratio and Rochester Quadrajet carburetor, power output topped the magical 200hp figure (actually 240!).

In 1957 Oldsmobile introduced the awesome J-2 Golden Rocket powerplant which, with 371ci, provided an amazing 277 pounding ponies at the gas pedal. Needless to say, these big-block pounders gratefully gulped down the highest octane gas available. The J-2 was the kingpin of the Olds powerplant lineup that model year. Combine the model's dynamite looks and that J-2 powerplant, and you have a desired collectible.

Zero to sixty performance, though, languished in the ten-second category because of the excessive weight of the car.

The new performance creation sat the performance world on its heels. The J-2 mill drew breath through a six-pack (three two-barrel carbs). The unique sound of the six-pack became famous, but not as an Olds. The J-2 never attained the fame of the other tri-powers—namely the 406 Ford and 389 Pontiac. As is well known, a six-pack made the GTO famous. Too bad it didn't happen for the Oldsmobile.

There were actually two versions of the J-2 powerplant. The milder version was basically the standard 371 engine sporting a high-tech gasket set that boosted the compression ratio to 10:1. A competition version of the J-2 carried a high-lift cam, beefed-up internal parts, and racing pistons. Few of these mills made it to street vehicles. The horsepower was rated at a ground-pounding 312!

We're talking full race with either version. The J-2 was produced for one year only, and if you ever find one, grab it quickly, no matter what the condition.

Oldsmobile may have missed a bet not refining this powerplant and bringing it into the sixties muscle arena. It would have been a hit! This powerful

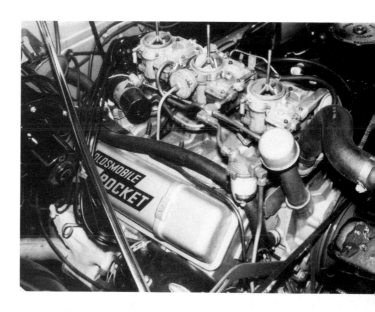

The J-2 powerplant. Would you believe 312hp and a tri-power setup? This was one of the first factory tri-carb setups, produced long before the Ford 406 and Pontiac 389.

mill could be ordered with any bodystyle.

We're not talking Indy Cars here, but another radical performance innovation was introduced by the infamous Dr. Olds in the late 1950s. Would you

A stylish elongated air cleaner was fitted over the triple carburetors of the 371ci J-2 engine. These rare powerplants were produced only in 1957.

An interesting early sixties experiment in Olds performance—a turbocharged engine. The engine used a modified 215ci Buick aluminum block.

believe a turbocharger? That was the idea, and the 215ci engine matched the mark of one-horsepower-per-cubic-inch set by Chevrolet's 283ci fuel-injected powerplant in 1957.

The engine was an aluminum 215ci Buick powerplant with Olds manifolds and heads. Little modification was required to adapt the engine to the turbo configuration. Changes included longer bearing caps, V-notched pistons, aluminized valve seats, and special main and connecting rod bearings. The interesting experiment resulted in a significant performance increase over the stock configuration.

The turbine was mounted to the intake manifold with a single-barrel Rochester carb feeding it. In order to counter high head temperatures and eliminate engine knock, a Turbo Rocket Fluid injection system containing distilled water and alcohol was employed. The fluid was carried in a five-quart bottle mounted on the inner fender. Zero-to-sixty performance was in the nine-second category. The vacuum-controlled waste gate was set to limit boost to

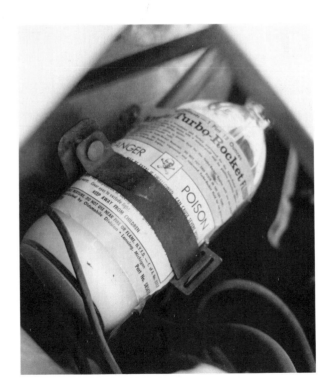

A five-quart bottle of Turbo Rocket Fluid was carried in the engine compartment to cool the high head temperatures produced by the turbo setup.

Turbo Rocket Fluid was carried in the engine compartment, mounted on an inner fender.

The 1961 Starfire was as close as Oldsmobile got to a muscle car in the early sixties. **Oldsmobile History Center**

five pounds per square inch.

The turbo-equipped F-85 was carried for two years (1962 and 1963) with a total of just 9,607 sold. Then it just faded away.

This was unfortunate because the powerplant was ahead of its time. Performance during that period came from carburetors and big cubic inches, and it wouldn't be until the eighties that the turbo would make itself felt.

Also during the early sixties came the Starfire model, a borderline muscle car. The horsepower started at 325 in 1961, moving to 345 in 1963, 370 in 1965, and finally, 375 in 1966.

So why didn't the Starfire ever gain the fame of its 442 brother? Well, quite frankly, the Starfire just didn't look like a muscle car. And as the sixties passed, the Starfire took on a more stately appearance.

The Starfire's changing image was accompanied

Even without the turbo setup, the 215ci small-block was still a powerful mill. With a four-barrel carburetor, it produced an impressive 185hp.

13

The 1962 394ci Starfire powerplant got the job done with a 10.5:1 compression ratio and hydraulic lifters which enabled 345hp at 4600rpm and 440lb-ft of torque at 3200rpm. Every bit of horsepower was necessary to push about 4,400 pounds of machine.

by declining production figures, with sales peaking in 1962 and then dropping off until its demise in 1966. The muscular 442 probably influenced Starfire's demise.

During the mid-sixties, there were other muscle powerplants that could have evolved. Designer Gilbert Burrel created an experimental single-overhead-camshaft edition of the Rocket in 1966. Then, a double-overhead-camshaft, thirty-two-valve V-8 was built and tested in 1967, twenty years before similar technology was introduced for sale in Olds' Quad 4 engine. A 650hp aluminum twin-turbo V-8 was also developed for Can-Am racing in the late sixties.

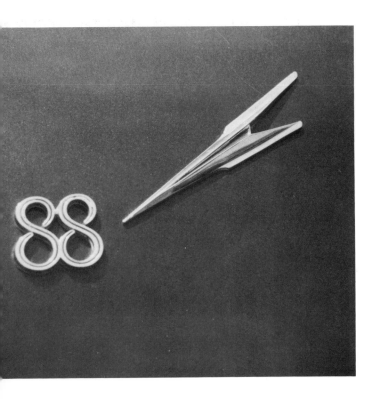

The rocket emblem acquired a sleeker appearance for the 1962 model year. The tail fins now stretched out, as compared to the stubby fins of earlier years.

The 1964 Jetstar ads promoted muscle. Although the Starfire boasted great styling and 345hp under the hood, muscle-car performance would never be the Jetstar's forte. **Oldsmobile advertisement**

The early sixties Olds muscle cars were great looking, all the way down to the wheel covers! This flashy unit was available on the 1964 models.

The top-gun Olds performance powerplant for 1966 was this 425ci Super Rocket powerplant which sported a 10.5:1 compression ratio and an amazing 375hp. It carried the Rochester 4GC four-barrel carb, five main bearings, and hydraulic lifters.

Since we're addressing any Olds that can be called a muscle car, there's one more model that must be mentioned; the Olds Toronado. You must be kidding, you say? That was an executive's prestige car, wasn't it? Well, that may be the popular perception, but its styling and performance make the Toronado a candidate for muscle recognition.

Of course, the unique fastback design of the 1966–1967 Toronados was big-time heavy, approaching 4,400 pounds. But Oldsmobile—through the guiding genius of Engineer Andy Watt—saw fit to bolt a massive 425ci powerplant to the T's frame.

With 385bhp in place, Toronado performance was surprisingly impressive showing 8.5 seconds in the zer-to-sixty mph run and a top speed over 130mph.

In 1968, the big-bore powerplant -Toronado combination showed that there was still plenty of life left in Oldsmobile performance when a Toronado won its class at the challenging Pikes Peak Hill Climb.

But even with all these muscular models, most Olds fans (and many Olds experts too) mistakenly believe that the Olds muscle era began when the 442 was introduced in 1964. But as has been noted, that wasn't the case. Olds muscle was around long before the famed 442 showed up.

Weighing some 4,400 pounds, it was stretching the truth to call the classy Toronado a muscle car. But it had some power under the hood—the twin-snorkel-topped 425ci mill pumped out an impressive 385 horses.

Chapter 2

The 442

It was an era of numbers for the muscle car set. The cars of the day were known by three-digit numbers that flaunted the cubic inches of the giant power-plants they carried, such as SS396, 421HO, 440 Six-Pack, and so on.

Naming the car after the engine displacement was the trend of the times, but GM's Oldsmobile division was the exception to the rule. Not that their muscle entry didn't have the required numbering; it did, with numerals that looked about right to be engine displacement numbers.

In Olds lingo, though, "442" meant something entirely different. Each digit had a specific meaning. It went like this: The first digit (four) stood for the four-barrel carb, the second identified the four-speed full-synchronized floor-mounted transmission, and that elusive two quite simply stood for the stock dual-exhaust system.

Even though the 442 probably never got the publicity of the other muscle machines of the period, it certainly lasted longer. And even after the punch had departed the engine compartment, the 442 nomenclature remained basically an appearance package, recalling earlier days when it was a performance machine.

The 442 was a legend, but there were several performance mutations of the model, including the W machines which added extra body detailing along with some extra ponies under the hood. There were also pace car models that carried the identification of

the Memorial Day Brickyard race and the famous Hurst models.

But this chapter will cover the *basic* 442, and its performance history through the years. The other versions are addressed later in the book.

1964

The initial 442s, surprisingly, had only 330ci, but before the 442 performance era ended, the displace-

Although small when compared to its brethren, the 330ci of the first 442 powerplant punched out impressive performance. There was no missing this mill, which was characterized by its bright orange air cleaner and the unique alignment of the 442 numbers. The 330ci of displacement would be kicked up to 400 for 1965.

The 442 was introduced in 1964 as the B-09 option available on the Cutlass. Many never figured out that those magical numbers—442—stood for four-barrel carburetor, four-on-the-floor transmission, and dual exhaust. In the years to follow, not all 442s carried those attributes, but the popular designation was still used.

Production figures were low for the 442 in its first year, with only 2,999 constructed. Performance of the 330ci power-plant was rated at an impressive 310bhp. This was just the beginning for an Olds model that enjoyed great success in the late sixties and early seventies.

ment would top 442 by 13ci.

The first 442 appeared in 1964, but its introduction was a bit strange to say the least. What the Olds management had in mind is still somewhat of a mystery. The youth market was the obvious target, but for some reason, the first 442 was advertised as a four-door police package, with two stern-looking cops behind the wheel, undoubtedly looking for "civilian" versions of their machine being tested on the street. The early advertisements stated, "Police wanted it…Olds built it…Pursuit proved it. Put this one on your wanted list!"

Along with the Men in Blue connotation, the ads flaunted the 310hp and 355lb-ft of torque from the four-barrel 330ci Jetfire Rocket V-8. The powerplant showed a 20hp increase over the previous 330ci mills, and that extra power paid big dividends in perfor-

The hood for the first 442 was clean as a whistle, but that trend did not continue. Later models featured scoops and flashy striping. But this 442, which was nothing more than an F-85 performance option, set the trend for years to come.

The design of that first 442 was relatively clean and simple. It was accentuated by a chrome strip that ran the length of the body.

mance. Reportedly, the zero-to-sixty time was in the mid-seven-second range.

The punchy powerplant sported a 3.94in bore, 3.38in stroke, and hydraulic lifters. Sporting a 10.25:1 compression ratio and a downdraft four-barrel carburetor, the powerplant set the performance trend for the magnificent 442 mills to follow.

Other performance goodies mentioned in the advertisements included "track-tested Red-Line tires and heavy-duty chassis components." Oldsmobile also sang praises about the 442's excellent handling. Heavy-duty springs up front were rated at 410 pounds while the rating out back was 160 pounds. In addition, there were beefy front and rear stabilizer bars. For its time, the 442 handled superbly, with a firmer ride than most of the muscle car competition of the time.

A September 1964 *Motor Trend* test of a 1964 442 coupe showed that the first 442 was a performer,

Chrome detailing was evident on the body of the first 442. As seen here, a chrome strip traversed the lower body and inside the wheel opening edge.

The B-09 performance option was derived from a police interceptor package, and can be credited for bringing Oldsmobile into the muscle car arena in the mid-sixties.

The rear-end of the 1964 442 was simple, yet elegant. The design featured matching triple rear lens lights that were joined by a chrome stripe bearing the 442 name.

The heritage of the first 442 was carried on the front quarters and on the lower right rear deck. With minimal quantities of this model produced, it has become an exciting collectible.

This sporty wire wheel with simulated knock-off hub was an attractive addition to the first 442.

A prominent feature of the 1965 442 was this behind-the-door cutout bearing a multi-colored 442 emblem. The cubic inches moved up 70 to a pounding 400ci for the 442's second year.

The body design of the second 442 in 1965 changed little from the initial model. The rear-end was revised, and the 442 identification was missing from the rear deck.

The wheel for the second 442 was a bit sportier, with a three-pronged knock-off hub.

rating 7.5 seconds in the zero-to-sixty mph test. With a four-speed tranny, the 442 topped out at 116mph. Not bad when you consider that the test car had a curb weight of 3,440 pounds!

Surprisingly, the first 442 was not a separate model, but an option package for the F-85 Cutlass line. The performance-minded buyer could opt for the B-09 option, otherwise known as the Police Pursuit Apprehender package, for an additional $289.14.

The 442 option was available with any F-85 model, except station wagons. The Cutlass hardtop coupe (body style #127) was the most popular model to get the 442 numbering, with 1,842 produced. Next came the Cutlass coupe (#227) at 563, along with 436 Cutlass convertibles. With the total of only 2,999 produced that year, finding one of these models in the nineties could be difficult and expensive.

Of that total, only ten four-door sedans were built that model year, which is understandable. Those who preferred the muscular 442 performance image, and those who were looking for a nice four-door family car were two different breeds. But finding one of those 442 sedans would be a kick!

1965

With the superb publicity the initial 442 acquired, it was not surprising that Olds engineers would kick up the ponies a bit the following year. All the 1964 goodies were still in place, but the 330ci powerplant was replaced with a ground-pounding 400ci, 345hp mill.

Both the bore and stroke increased to a 4.00 inch bore and 3.98 inch stroke. The compression ratio remained extremely high at 10.25:1.

The new 400ci engine was topped with a 700cfm Quadrajet carburetor and carried a special radiator, 70amp battery, and dual low-restriction exhaust.

This second-year 442 performed like a champ on the 1,320 foot strips! The car magazines proclaimed the model's performance virtues, and the buying public responded by purchasing 25,003 442s that year.

The 442 option was now officially identified as the W-29, a practice continued through the 1967 model year. The standard 442 was, in effect, the first

"W" car, an identification Olds would later use in performance machines. Again, the option cost only $156.02.

Hooked up with a special driveshaft and performance rear axle, the 1965 machine was a real mover. But frankly, the second 442 was a poor comparison

If the wires were a little wild for your liking, you could have this very staid design. It also might help disguise the performance machine upon which they were mounted.

The 442 identification moved to the left side of the slightly revised grill for 1965. The Oldsmobile name was contained in a bar that split the grill.

The standard powerplant for 1966 was the same 400ci unit, although horsepower was up 5 to 350. A 442 equipped with this powerplant was a solid performer, with quarter-mile times approaching fourteen seconds.

Top right
The killer, the blunderbuss. Call it what you like, the special one-year L-69 tri-power engine got the attention of the performance-minded. The L-69 put ten additional horses and a lot of charisma under the hood. A few of these powerhouses were ordered with the rare W-30 ram air induction option.

with the muscular offerings from its fellow General Motors divisions. As part of its performance image, the powerplant was available only with the four-speed transmission.

Externally the 1965 442 changed slightly from the premier model, being 1.4 inches longer than the original. The Oldsmobile name was now carried in the center horizontal grill bar. The main identifier, though, was a simulated air scoop just aft of the front door rear seam. The optional wire wheels really set off this model's appearance.

Under the hood was a chrome air cleaner bearing the lettering "Ultra High Compression" and a three-color 442 emblem. Not surprisingly, a majority of the buyers (13,735) selected the four-speed transmission, with 10,578 picking the automatic.

From a collector's point of view, an original second-year 442 would be a real find, but with only a

Bottom right
The 442 identification for the 1966 model was carried in several places, including the left side of the grill recess and the rear quarter. The rear quarter cutout with the 442 numbers was missing this year.

Sales for this 1966 model were slightly off the previous year's figures. A total of 21,997 were sold, with the Cutlass hardtop coupe being the most popular model with 13,493 sold.

few produced almost three decades ago, it certainly won't be easy.

1966

In 1966, a name problem arose when an optional L-69 three two-barrel (300cfm each) carb setup was offered. Oldsmobile didn't call it a 642, though. Introduced two years after the Pontiac GTO tri-power setup, the 442 3-2 setup never attracted as much attention. Only a few of these interesting muscle mills were factory-built, but a number more were retrofitted by dealers and owners. Wouldn't you have done it at the time?

The setup used three two-barrel Carter carbure-

Performance was key to the advertising campaign for the 1967 model, as evidenced by this December 1966 ad. The long list of equipment available makes the 1967 442 sound like a full-race machine. This was an exciting machine!
Oldsmobile advertisement

The standard powerplant for the 1967 442 was this awesome 400ci, 350hp mill that pounded a brutish 440lb-ft of torque at 3600rpm. When equipped with a Turbo 400 transmission and the appropriate rear-end gearing, you had one hot street and strip performer.

tors on a special manifold. Nothing else in the 442 engine was changed. The center carb was used for normal driving and the other two were brought on-line simultaneously by a progressive linkage setup. In the August 1966 issue, *Car Life* magazine raved about the operation of the system.

The L-69 tri-carb setup, built in 1966 only, provided an additional ten horses (360hp rating) over the standard four-barrel engine. An extremely rare W-30 ram air induction option could also be ordered, but we'll talk about that option in another chapter. A total of 2,169 L-69 versions were built for that model year. To vintage Olds lovers, this is one of the most desirable early Olds muscle machines.

The standard 442 powerplant was the 400ci mill, pumping out 350hp, five more than in 1965. Also, the compression ratio had been nudged to 10.5:1.

The 1967 442 was starting to look like a racer. The sheet metal had been slightly revised and was looking tough. And by the way, those louvers were factory, even though they looked like custom work done at a local speed shop.

The pressure to perform on street and strip was definitely having an effect under the hood of the third-year 442.

The 1966 442 could be ordered with five bodystyles. Production was still strong at 21,997, and the Holiday hardtop was the most popular seller.

The bodystyling changed slightly for 1966, with blacked-out tail panel and grill. The 442 emblems were prominently located on the right rear deck, rear quarter, and grill.

1967

Production of the 442 was up slightly in 1967 to 24,829 (topped by 16,996 hardtops). Five different bodystyles would be equipped with the 442 option this model year. Not surprisingly, almost two-thirds of

the buyers selected the four-speed transmission.

The 442 for 1967 was beginning to gain a distinctive look with a unique grill embedded with a 442 emblem. The characteristic fender scoops were gone for this year, but the model did sport pinstriping on the doors and fenders. The look was set off with red-line tires.

Troy Varney is a big 442 fan who owns a number of the flashy vintage machines. His 1967 model is interesting because Varney has documented that this particular car was a participant in the 1967 Miss America Contest Parade. "Miss Oklahoma rode in the car," Varney explains. "Another interesting fact about this car is that it was the only 442 among the parade cars, all the others being Cutlass convertibles."

Varney, a heavy equipment operator, came across the car while digging a basement for the car's first owner. "The guy explained that he went to the dealer right after the parade and bought it," Varney says. It wasn't long before Troy convinced the guy that he should sell it. The louvers on the hood might have looked like they were fashioned by some street rodder, but rest assured, they were definitely fabricated at the factory. The model also incorporated front quarter pinstriping to great appearance advantage.

The tri-carb setup was officially gone for 1967, but the 440lb-ft of torque and 350hp four-barrel engine remained in place. The powerhouse mill was still perking at a 10.5:1 compression ratio with hydraulic valve lifters.

Also, powertrain upgrades allowed the awesome engine to operate at much greater efficiency. A special Turbo Hydra-Matic transmission, a stronger twelve-bolt rear end (available with 3.42 and 3.91 ratios), and F70xl4 wide ovals made the 1967 442 a street performer of the first order. The automatic outsold the four-speed for the first time (13,528 to 11,381).

The 442 was also starting to turn heads on the national drag strips in 1967, and set a B/Pure Stock national record.

Even though the 442 was working on achieving a muscle image, an interesting economy option was offered in 1967. The Turnpike Cruiser option (L-65), used a two-barrel carb, a conservative transmission, and an altered rear-end gear ratio. The popular option provided greater economy with just a minor decrease in power. Horsepower was down sixty ponies, with only a 15lb-ft drop in torque. It was a nice combination of performance and economy. As with the tri-

One of the best features of the 1967 442 became apparent when the machine was pulling away. The stacked taillights were separated by a blacked-out rear panel with a multi-colored 442 designation on the lower right corner of the rear deck.

The distinctive grill design of the 1967 442 featured separated twin headlights and an embedded 442 emblem on the left side of the grill.

carb setup in 1966, the 442 name stayed the same even though it should have been changed to 242 to be totally correct. In its February 1967 issue, *Motor Trend* rated the economy version above the standard four-barrel model.

Charlie Shaudys is the owner of many Olds performance cars. Shaudys says that his Turnpike Cruiser-equipped model is one of his favorites. He claims that the option doesn't noticeably downgrade performance.

1968

For 1968, the news was big in the 442 camp for two reasons. First, the 442 became a separate model rather than just an F-85 option. Second, the entire

Olds line was redesigned, and the 442 received a new bodystyle and a three inch shorter wheelbase (112 inches). The December 1967 issue of *Motor Trend* described the 1968 442 as a "stirring car, full of built-ins and potential for performance enthusiasts."

The 400ci engine was still under the hood for 1968, but bore increased to 4.125 inches and stroke diminished to 3.385 inches. Horsepower was quoted at 350 with the four-speed and 325 with the automatic.

Harvey Freeman has an immaculately-restored 1968 442. He's had the beauty since 1982. "When I got the car, it was simply terrible. Somebody had painted it with a roller! I paid $450 for the hulk and it was certainly no bargain at the price. The initial plan was to use it as a parts car, but I kind of got attached to it. You know how those things go." Freeman explains that only the W-30 models came stock with the vertical Ralley Stripes. "They cost you an extra $15, $80 if you wanted them on a 442," he

Top left
The 1967 442 featured this body-length metal crease. Both the front and rear bumpers were molded into the body.

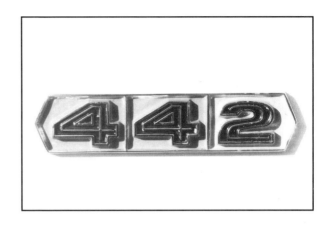

adds.

Freeman recalls an incident that took place just after the car was painted. "We had just put a cover over the car when some kids playing ball nearby hit a ball through the garage window. The resulting broken glass fell down on the cover, cutting it, and

Bottom left
The 1967 442 carried body identification numbers on the lower rear deck, front quarters, and grill. The Olds rocket symbol was mounted on the rear quarters. Dual exhaust poked out below the rear bumper.

No doubt about the identification of the 1967 442. The bold numbers were there for all to see, and a lot of performance buyers liked what they saw with this hauler.

The look of the 1967 442 front end is best described as classy. Twin headlights were separated by the parking light, and the 442 identification is clearly evident from this view.

A tachometer was one of the many performance options available with the 1967 442.

messing up the paint underneath. It broke my heart." But things are obviously back in place.

A 400ci powerplant, perking at a 10.5:1 compression ratio and equipped with a four-barrel Quadrajet carb, produced 325hp at 4800rpm and 440lb-ft of torque at only 3200rpm. The low thunder from the dual exhaust expresses those numbers.

The model has a distinct appearance, with 442 numerals centered on a macho-looking blacked-out grill. The numbers also appear on the mid front quarters and lower right rear deck, while the Olds emblems are centered on the rear deck and rear quarters. The new blacked-out slotted wheels accented the 1968's new swoopy bodystyling.

The buying public liked what it saw in the redesigned 442, with 36,641 buyers making the purchase.

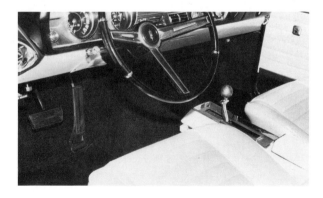

For its time, the 1967 442 carried one of the best-looking interiors around. A combination of luxury and sporty styling, the model featured buckets and a console-mounted shifter.

1969

The overall body lines of the 1969 442 didn't change that radically for the final model of the decade, but there was a considerably different look to the front end. The grill was halved by body-colored sheet metal scribed with the 442 identification. The 442 numerals were boldly blocked out on the front quarters and flaunted on the rear deck.

The rear of the '69 model sported redesigned taillights rotated ninety degrees to a vertical position. The 400ci powerplant was bumped up to 350hp and was unforgettable in appearance.

The air cleaner was painted bright red which assured that there was no missing this sprightly engine compartment. The suspension was up to handling those oh-so-plentiful ponies. These models carried beefy front and rear sway bars along with heavy-duty springs and shocks. Equipped with the M-21 close-ratio four-speed transmission and 3.23 limited-slip rear end, this 442 could hold its head high against anything offered by the competition.

In the nineties, it seems that the more glamorous W machines and Hurst modifications get all the glory, but the styling and performance of the 1969 basic 442 merits collector appreciation. The basic 442 for this model year was an excellent seller, with 29,839 rolling from the showroom floor.

1970

The 1970 442 body design was slightly altered and projected a more refined look. The rear bumper now carried four slotted vertical taillights located directly over the stylish dual-exhaust extensions and an optional rear-deck-mounted W-35 spoiler.

There were also refinements to the front end with a new vertical pattern in the twin grill. Next came macho hood scoops in the W-25 hood; the neat thing was that they were functional! A pair of racing-style hood pins also served their intended purpose. It's easy to understand why many 442 fans will tell you it didn't get much better than the 1970 model. Again, production was considerably off from the previous year with only 19,330 produced. Was this the beginning of the end for performance?

More ponies under the hood matched the 1970's new look. The cubic inches hit 455 with a 4.125 inch bore and a 4.250 inch stroke. Horsepower was an impressive 365 (at 5000rpm). Torque was up to a stump-pulling 500lb-ft (one of the highest

Right
Cars *magazine voted the 1968 442 as the Top Performance Car of the Year, and it was well deserved. The power train appeared ready to run at Daytona right off the showroom floor. Heavy-duty suspension was accompanied by front and rear stabilizers and wide oval redline tires.* **Oldsmobile advertisement.**

Olds 4·4·2: Here's what's behind the reputation.

ENGINE

Type.........................Rocket V-8
Bore x stroke, inches........3.87 x 4.25
Displacement, cubic inches........400
Compression ratio.............10.5-to-1
Bhp...................350* at 4800 rpm
Torque, lb.-ft...........440 at 3200 rpm
Carburetion........................4-bbl.
Exhausts..........................Dual
　Built-in Combustion Control System provides constant carb air temperature.
　Availabilities: Force-Air Induction System. 360 bhp at 5400 rpm. Teams with close-ratio 4-on-the-floor transmission or Turbo Hydra-Matic.
　Cruising package: Includes 400-CID V-8 with 2-bbl. carb, 290 bhp, 9-to-1 compression, Turbo Hydra-Matic, 2.56-to-1 axle.
*325-hp Rocket 400 V-8 with 4-bbl. carb and 10.5-to-1 compression ratio teams with Turbo Hydra-Matic.

DRIVE TRAIN

Transmission.......Fully synchronized, heavy-duty 3-on-the-floor with Hurst Shifter
　Availabilities: 4-on-the-floor (close- or wide-ratio with Hurst Shifter) or Turbo Hydra-Matic floor shift.
Prop shaft...................Heavy-duty
Axle ratios.....2.56-to-1 up to 4.66-to-1
　Availabilities: Heavy-duty axles (H.D. shafts, bearings, differential gears), 3 ratios.

CHASSIS

Suspension.......Heavy-duty. Includes heavy-duty springs and shocks, front and rear stabilizers.
Steering ratio....................24-to-1
Wheels.............Heavy-duty 14-inch with extra-wide rims
Tires.............F70 x 14", Nylon-Cord Wide-Oval Red-Lines

OTHER AVAILABILITIES

Power front disc brakes. UHV Transistorized Ignition. Anti-Spin Differential. Rally Stripes. Rally Pac (clock, tach, engine gauges). Sports console. Custom Sport Steering Wheel. Simulated-wire and Super Stock Wheels. Special wheel discs. Others.

GENERAL

Wheelbase.........................112"
Overall length...................201.6"
Overall width.....................76.2"
Overall height....................52.8"
Curb wt. (lb.) Holiday Coupe......3670
Tread...........front 59.0", rear 59.0"

SAFETY

All the new GM safety features are standard, including energy-absorbing column, seat belts for all passenger positions.

CARS Magazine names Olds 4-4-2 "Top Performance Car of the Year."

Top left
The standard powerplant for the 1968 442 was a super street and strip performer, kicking out 325bhp from 400ci. With a 10.5:1 compression ratio, four-barrel carburetor, and dual exhaust, this engine was one of the top performers of its time.

Right
The hood design had been altered considerably for 1968. This hood-length bulge was right in line with the 442's new look.

amounts ever).

Plenty of options were available to dress up this heavy hauler. The M-40 Turbo Hydra-matic with the W-26 Hurst Dual Gate Shifter was a killer combination for street or strip. The FE2 sport suspension was also state of the art. Cosmetic options for the 1970 442 included the D-35 Sport Mirrors, the N-34 Custom Sport Steering Wheel, and N-66 Super Stock Wheels.

Oldsmobile ads at the time touted the first 442 of the decade. "Beneath that air scooped, fiberglass hood rumbles as large a V-8 as ever has been bolted into a special performance, production automobile...The special hood? It's part of the new W-25 package you can order. Do so—while you're still young enough to enjoy it!"

The only mystery is why the production of this magnificent hauler was so far off the previous year. Again, it probably was one of the first signs of the decline of the muscle era. The hardtop coupe once again was the resounding favorite with 14,709 sold.

Was the love of performance waning in America? One generally held belief was that potential young male buyers were being shuttled off, or worrying about going to Vietnam. Maybe the war took the edge off the country's hunger for hot cars. But how

Bottom left
Dynamite! That was the best way to describe the new 442 body design for 1968. Everything was new in the three-inch-shorter hauler. This particular convertible is set off with an optional vertical front quarter stripe at the 442 numerals.

It might have been a Hurst aftermarket shifter, but the engraved 442 numbers verified that it was a factory installation. It certainly made hot rod enthusiasts happy!

The 442 numbers stood out like never before in the 1968 442's bold black background. Many consider this design the most attractive of all the muscle-era 442s.

The large chrome 442 numerals on this 1969 model touted the machine's performance. The 442 was making its mark during this time period.

Left
The modified hood design of the 1969 442 lasted for a number of years. The twin humps stretched the entire length of the hood, with pinstriping if you desired.

The sporty interior of the 1968 442 had 442 ID plaques mounted on the glove box door, bucket seats, and on the classy sport steering wheel. A Hurst shifter mounted in the center console.

could anybody resist this magnificent machine? This 442 was about as good as it got!

1971

Apparently the Oldsmobile division started to back away from performance, as evidenced by the downward spiral of the 442's tire-scorching capabilities. But don't get the idea that it was just Oldsmobile responding to the "performance turn-off" in America. The trend affected the entire automotive industry.

The 442 was still in place for 1971, but production was down. In previous years, 442s accounted for as much as 5 to 6 percent of total production for the auto maker. In 1971, though, the 7,589 442s produced accounted for only 1.3 percent of Oldsmobile production.

These attractive wheels gave the 442 a sporty, racing look. The design featured five spokes radiating from an Olds-emblazoned center hub with five chrome lug bolts.

Pinstriping on the hood accentuated the styling of the 1969 442. The two hood bulges were highlighted; they would become functional air scoops in the years to come.

The 1971 442 didn't look that much different from the preceding model year. That rakish twin-scoop hood, complete with the hood pins, was still in place, and there was a modified mesh grill pattern (that was the only significant external change). Major powerplant changes, though, were taking place across the industry. The culprit was low-octane unleaded fuel–something that high-compression engines didn't care for one bit! Also, government-mandated pollution controls clamped down on performance. In the words of Bob Dylan, "The times, they were a-changing!"

In order to safely burn the low octane gas, it was necessary for Olds—along with all the other GM divisions—to drop compression two full digits. That's a bunch, and it's amazing the horsepower didn't drop more than it did. The 455 powerplant dropped a minimal 25 horses to a still-impressive 340hp. It would be the final year that horsepower would be quoted in gross horsepower numbers.

An interesting change for 1971 was that an Olds symbol replaced the 442 numbers on the center grill bar. The numbers moved to the left grill mesh, which was a slap in the face for the performance image of the 442.

Jack Kerr has one of the best 1971 442s in the nation, a car that won its class in the 1993 Olds Nationals. This Viking Blue beauty is loaded with an M-40 Turbo 400 Hydra-matic transmission, dealer-installed aluminum differential cover, luxury interior, and much more.

This was not a recent acquisition for Kerr, but a long-time love affair. He's had the car since 1975, when he was a senior in high school.

"It just sort of sat while I went to college and got into work. On my fifteenth high school reunion, I drove it and blew them away again...That's when I

The 1970 442. In their ads, Olds called it the "Complete Escape Machine." With its pounding (and brand-new) 455 powerplant, it was seen escaping the competition in more than one drag race. The new grill and W-25 hood could also be ordered with this redesigned muscle machine. Oldsmobile advertisement.

Beneath that air-scooped, fiberglass hood rumbles as large a V-8 as ever bolted into a special-performance, production automobile.

Olds 4-4-2: The complete Escape Machine. The name of the game is cubic inches. 4-4-2 packs 455 of them, standard! But this V-8 is more than big. It's revolutionary. It features Olds' exclusive Positive Valve Rotators for smoother, more trouble-free performance. Something else that's news—the 4-4-2 suspension with front *and rear* stabilizers. The imitators are popping up faster than you can say "me too." The special hood? It's part of the new W-25 package you can order. Do so—while you're still young enough to enjoy it!

decided to do a complete frame-off restoration." Kerr says the restoration on the beautiful 442 will never be completed. "I plan to keep working on it 'til it can't get any better," he explains.

1972

In 1972, it seemed that "performance" was a dirty word. The trend was evident in Oldsmobile's advertisements–engine performance was in small print.

The 1972 442 was advertised as "a special 442 Sport Handling Package," which could be ordered on four different Cutlass models. Those included the hardtop coupe, two Cutlass S Coupes, and the Cutlass Supreme convertible.

The term "package" was used once again in the ads, indicating some bad news for the 442. After four years of being offered as a separate model, the 442 was back to the W-29 option.

To garb your 1972 as a 442, though, was inexpensive; $71.62 for the Cutlass and $150.61 for the Cutlass Supreme. Both included the Hurst three-speed shifter.

The package also included body and rear deck striping, louvers, and the expected trio of famous numbers. Suspension pieces (carried under the FE Rallye Suspension Package) were heavy-duty springs and shocks, front and rear stabilizer bars, heavy-duty rear lower control arms, and I4x7 inch tires. Olds wasn't getting out of the performance business, but the trend was well under way.

New government regulations, high insurance rates for big-engined cars, and the trend toward lower-cost cars had automotive designers looking in different directions. The 1972 442 still performed well, but it was starting to feel the pressure.

Subtle body changes reflected the more conservative times. The new grill didn't carry the rakish lines of its predecessors, while the body shaping was smoother and more "domestic." The new taillights were an egg-crate design, with six light openings separated by a vertical bar.

The standard 1972 442 powerplant (the L-75) was rated at 270nhp. Remember, those were *net* horses, so the reduction wasn't as bad as it appeared. Brake horsepower was probably close to 300.

This driver-side-mounted thermometer was an option on the 1971 442. The device mounted just forward of the outside mirror.

They were bulging and functional. The color-striped hood scoops on the 1971 442 got the job done, but power-increasing devices such as this were on their way out.

Even in this era of downgrading performance 445ci were still in place under the hood. Amazingly, those cubic inches would be available through the 1976 model year.

Torque was still plentiful, though, with 370lb-ft (net) which equated to over 400 on the gross rating table. Once again, these are impressive figures from a minimal 8.5:1 compression ratio, even though the mill did carry dual exhaust and a four-barrel carburetor.

The 455 engine was a special order for the 442, the standard engines being two 350ci engines, with very un-muscle-car-like net horsepower ratings of 160 and 180. Sad what those famous 442 numbers were coming to! You could still deck out your 1972 442, however, in muscle-car-like add-ons with the Super Stock II wheels and Rallye Pak instrumentation.

The 442 option was available in the F-37 Cutlass

The addition of hood locks became popular in the late sixties, and 442s had been wearing them since 1969. This is one of two that were carried on the forward portion of the hood on the 1971 442.

This 1971 442 could be considered the final big-block muscle car. Its horsepower was slightly reduced, but its mill was still capable of 340hp at 4600rpm.

A 1971 442 during a restoration build-up. The big-block filled the engine compartment to the hilt.

hardtop coupe (360 built) and the classy G-37 Cutlass S hardtop coupe (9,777). There were also 1,171 442-equipped Cutlass S convertibles constructed. A 1971 model with a 455 engine under the hood would make an economical restoration project.

1973

It's hard to determine exactly when a model is no longer considered a true muscle car, but the 1973 442 was approaching that status.

The gas crunch was starting and economy was getting the nod over sporty looks and performance. The trend was set in the early seventies and by 1973, the industry was getting serious. There were no convertibles for this model year, but the superficial 442

Right
The flashy 442 benefited from the classic body sculpturing vividly illustrated here. The 442 block numbers appeared on the rear deck, front quarter, and on the left-side grill meshing.

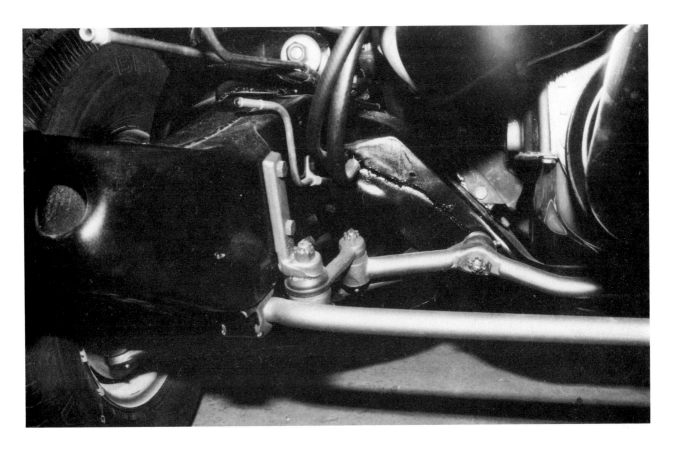

A view of the 1971 442 suspension system as you've never seen it before. The beefy components are capable of handling the heavy horses topside.

It was a sign of the times when the infamous 442 ceased to be a separate model in 1972. It was now a sport/handling package that could be ordered on several different models. These models still had the 442's macho looks, but they didn't have much under the hood. Oldsmobile advertisement.

option remained.

The 442 look could be acquired in either the Cutlass or Cutlass S coupes. The 442 package (which added a minimal cost of $121 to the sticker price) didn't include any special powerplant. That choice was up to the buyer.

Two highly-detuned versions of the 455 were available, but both were a far cry from their earlier 10.5:1 compression ratio brethren. Buyers could choose from the L-77 270nhp and L-75 250nhp versions, which performed impressively under low-compression constraints.

The 442 production total for the 1973 model year was 10,137, the highest since 1970, and a production peak not to be topped until 1977.

The 442 option package for 1973 consisted of heavy-duty suspension, a custom grill design, pinstriping, 442 identification, and a fake-louvered hood. It all looked good, and the 442 performance enthusiast could dream.

1974

Performance-minded enthusiasts were saddened again in 1974, when the L-75 455ci big-block was downgraded once more to an anemic 230 net horses. Other powertrain options included the Hurst-shifted four-speed and 3.42-geared limited–slip rear axle. The production total dropped off to 7,204, but the worst production numbers yet to come for the 442. The 442 package could be ordered (by specifying the W-29 option) for only $58!

1975 and 1976

The fact that the 455 was still available through 1976 is probably the only reason these models should even be included in the muscle category. The 455 was castrated, but the L-74 version was still around. Production totals for the two model years were 6,227 and 9,576, respectively.

The 442 option was still ordered under the W-29 nomenclature in 1975, costing a mere $128. It could

Two 350ci powerplants were available with the 1972 442, with horsepower ratings of 160 and 180nhp. Remember, though, those are net *ratings so they're not quite as low as they might appear.*

Right
The 1972 model had the same basic lines as the previous model years but it just didn't seem as rakish looking. An impressive FE handling package eased the pain of the performance downgrade.

be ordered with both the G-37 and F-37 Cutlass models, with the former being by far the more popular selection. Again, there was no standard powerplant for the 442. In fact, you could order *any* engine with the 442, which probably means there are a number of six-cylinder versions wearing the once-proud numbers.

For 1976, the 442 option was just a handling package, but it's presence was announced in huge block letters on the door panel. Available only on the G-37 Cutlass, the $134 W-29 option included heavy-duty shocks and springs, seven-inch wheels, and beefy sway bars. Again, you could order any powerplant that struck your fancy.

1977

For 1977, the 442 identification was flaunted with the same huge numbers on the lower door, along with a sloped aerodynamic nose, a configuration that would be used in NASCAR racing. The 455 big-block was gone, but there was a new 403 cubic incher that provided a lukewarm 180nhp. The emphasis for the 442 option, as in the previous year, was strictly suspension and flashy graphics.

"Performance" just did not apply to the 1972 442. Car makers were using words like "handling" and "economy." The 1972 example still looked good but packed less horsepower underneath the high-performance hood.

Top Left
The standard powerplant for the 1972 442 was still capable of 270hp, certainly nothing to scoff at, but it was on a downward spiral from the earlier powerhouse numbers. It still had great looks, though.

Since there was no special performance Hurst/Olds model (see Chapter 4) for this model year, this was the only way to go if you wanted even the *suggestion* of performance. Once again, the G-37 Cutlass S hardtop was the only model to receive the W-29 package, with some 11,649 being produced, the largest number during the seventies. Finding one of these models shouldn't be too difficult, and it would make an interesting collectible.

1978

The 442 powerplant was downsized in 1978, and again, the attention was on appearance and suspension. The appeal of those famous numbers declined as only 2,518 were sold. The option was available on the Cutlass S hardtop and Cutlass Brougham hardtop coupe.

Three engines were available with the 442; a 305ci Chevy V-8, a 231ci Buick V-6 , and a 260ci Olds V-6. None of the powerplants approached the fire once equated with the 442.

1979

In 1979, the big 442 plastered on the door was accompanied by a multi-color side styling. The numbers were also announced on the lower rear deck. The option included a number of suspension modifications (including sway bars and heavy-duty springs and shocks), along with a special grill.

In that last year of the seventies, 442 production hit rock bottom: only 620 were built, with the same two models receiving the option. The LG4 four-barrel five-liter Chevy was the top powerplant, and, hooked up with a four-speed, it made a pretty good high-per-

The Super Stock II wheels were still around for appearance-minded buyers in 1972. They set off the 442 in a big way!

Bottom left
How'd you like this brutish front end staring you in the face? The 1972 442 still looked tough, with its characteristic split grill and stylish but nonfunctional scoops.

The 1972 442 was an option rather than a separate model. The 442 trademark was clearly visible on the lower right corner of the rear deck. This styling remains popular in the nineties.

On the 1972 442, the famous numbers were carried on the egg-crate grill. Performance was fading, but the numbers were still in place.

formance package–for the time, that is!

1980

1980 was the final production year for the 442 for a number of years, and the 442 was much the same as the previous year. Sales weren't much better (with only 886 sold), and the 442 option (now called the W-30 Option O) was available only with the K-47 Cutlass Calais hardtop coupe. With such a poor reception, it wasn't surprising that the model was dropped after this model year.

The interior of the 1972 442 was neat and functional. Note that the 442 numbering appeared in the wood grain panel of the glove box door. The center console was contoured to blend with the floor, and contained the floor shifter.

Final Disposition

The 442 identification appeared on several different models in the eighties, but it wasn't the same. Ah, for those glorious days of the sixties and early seventies! That was a time when the 442 badge signified *performance*.

Oldsmobile 442 Production Totals

(*Note:* Figures do not include W-equipped cars.)

1964 (B-09 Option)

Model	Bodystyle	Production
027	F-85 club coupe	148
069	F-85 4-door sedan	3
169	F-85 Deluxe 4-door	7
227	Cutlass coupe	563
237	Cutlass hardtop coupe	1,842
267	Cutlass convertible	436
Total		2,999

1965 (W-29 Option)

3427	F-85 club coupe	1,087
3827	Cutlass coupe	5,713
3837	Cutlass hardtop coupe	14,735
3867	Cutlass convertible	3,468
Total		25,003

1966 (W-29 Option)

3407	F-85 club coupe	647
3617	F-85 hardtop coupe	1,217
3807	Cutlass coupe	3,787
3817	Cutlass hardtop coupe	13,493
3867	Cutlass convertible	3,468
Subtotal		21,997

(L-69 442)

3407	F-85 club coupe	157
3617	F-85 Deluxe hardtop coupe	178
3807	Cutlass coupe	383

For 1973, the Olds Cutlass line was completely redesigned and the 442 option looked quite different. Even though the car maker expected sales to go down, that didn't happen. Production was up slightly over the previous year at 10,137.

3817	Cutlass hardtop coupe	1,171
3867	Cutlass convertible	240
Subtotal		2,129
1966 Total		24,126

1967 (W-29 Option)
3807	Cutlass Supreme coupe	4,751
3817	Cutlass Supreme hardtop	16,998
3867	Cutlass Supreme convertible	3,080
Total		24,829

1968 (442 Model)
4467	442 convertible	5,142
4477	442 club coupe	4,726
4487	442 hardtop coupe	26,773
Total		36,641

1969 (442 Model)
4467	442 convertible	4,295
4477	442 club coupe	2,984
4487	442 hardtop coupe	22,560
Total		29,839

1970 (442 Model)
4467	442 convertible	2,933
4477	442 club coupe	1,688
4487	442 hardtop coupe	14,709
Total		19,330

1971 (442 Model)
4467	442 convertible	1,304
4487	442 hardtop coupe	6,285
Total		7,589

The front numerals were no longer in the grill, but instead were centered in the wide hood-length stripe. But frankly, it seemed that the 442 had lost its menacing look.

1972 (W-29 Option)

3287	Cutlass hardtop coupe	751
3677	Cutlass S club coupe	123
3687	Cutlass S hardtop coupe	7,800
4267	Cutlass S convertible	1,171
Total		9,845

1973 (W-29 Option)

F-37	Cutlass hardtop coupe	360
G-37	Cutlass S hardtop coupe	9,777
Total		10,137

1974 (W-29 Option)

F-37	Cutlass hardtop coupe	245
G-37	Cutlass S hardtop coupe	6,954
Total		7,204

The highly-detuned 350ci powerplant for the 1975 442. A downgraded 455 could be special ordered. Production for the year wasn't bad, at 6,227.

1975 (W-29 Option)

F-37	Cutlass hardtop coupe	212
G-37	Cutlass S hardtop coupe	6,015
Total		6,227

1976 (W-29 Option)

G-37	Cutlass S hardtop coupe	9,576

1977 (W-29 Option)

G-37	Cutlass S hardtop coupe	11,649

1978 (W-29 Option)

87	Cutlass S hardtop coupe	1,380
J87	Cutlass B hardtop coupe	1,138
Total		
		2,518

1979 (W-29 Option)

87	Cutlass S hardtop coupe	350
J87	Cutlass B hardtop coupe	270
Total		620

1980 (W-30 Option)

K-47	Cutlass Calais hardtop coupe	886

442 Powerplants (1964—1972)

Model Year	Cubic Inches	Hp/rpm
1964	330	290/4800
1965	400	345/4800
1966	400	350/5000
	400	360/5000 (L-69)
1967	400	350/5000
1968	400	290/4600 (2bbl)
	400	350/4800 (4-spd)
	400	325/4800 (auto)
1969	400	350/4800 (4-spd)
	400	325/4800 (auto)
	400	290/4600 (2bbl)
1970	455	365/5000 (W-34)
1971	455	340/4600
1972	455	270/4400 (net)

The punch had pretty well left the 442 for the 1975 model year, but you couldn't say the same about the machine's looks. The hood carried a flashy full-length stripe with five slots in the middle. A real looker, for sure!

Steep lines graced the rear end and rear window of the 1975 442. Note the paint detailing around the wheel cutouts. Oldsmobile

The identification of the 1976 442 was touted as never before. Check the size of those lower door numbers. The 442 W-29 option cost an additional $129, but it was an appearance package only. Oldsmobile History Center

Although the 1975 442 didn't have the rakish lines of its earlier muscle-bound brothers, the heavyweight hauler still showed a lot of class and style. The 442 numbers were still in place on the front quarters in bold block letters.

Stock car racers found the aerodynamic styling of the 1977 442 to their liking, and the model saw action in NASCAR competition. Unfortunately, there was no big-block power-plant available. **Oldsmobile History Center**

*That nifty sloping nose was just what the doctor ordered for
slashing through the air at high speeds. There weren't quite
as many horses as in the past, though, to push this model.*
Oldsmobile History Center

The aerodynamic front was gone in 1978, replaced by a vertical, squared-off front end that would be in position for a number of years. The 442 numbers were located on the doors and ran over both body colors. **Oldsmobile History Center**

Chapter 3

The W Option Packages

"**W**" was wild with the W–model Oldsmobiles of the late sixties and early seventies. The cars equipped with the W-30, W-31, and W-32 packages are some of the hottest Oldsmobiles ever produced. In the nineties, such W-modified machines are the most coveted and valuable of the Olds line. Initially, the "W" identification wasn't even visible on the car; but Oldsmobile quickly realized that identification should be announced for all to see and later models bore badges that indicated the powerful package's presence. With the initial W machines, it was necessary to lift the hood to ascertain the level of performance. Badges or no, these rare Olds muscle machines made their presence known. They definitely were in a class by themselves.

The W-30 Option

The W-30 was the most common of the three W options, and was available from 1966 to 1972. From an enthusiast's perspective, that twenty-first letter of the alphabet set the Olds apart from its competitors. Let's see exactly what the W-30 performance package consisted of through its seven years in existence.

1966 W-30

The 1966 442 was the first Olds to receive W hardware. The initial W-30 equipment could be ordered as a factory option or added to an existing powerplant. One high-powered example was the tri-carbed L-69 442 engine which surely didn't *need* any additional horses.

The W-30 package consisted of a ram air system, hotter cam, and stiffer valve springs. The induction system was a unique dual-snorkel air cleaner with a trio of twin-nut depressions. The five-inch-diameter air cleaner openings were attached to a pair of hoses that ran to openings in the front bumper. That way, cool outside air was fed directly to the carburetors. The in-

The W powerplant for 1967 was a killer, producing a ground-pounding 360hp, some 35hp more than the standard 442 400ci mill. The powerplant featured twin induction tubes, a 328 degree cam, and stiffer valve springs. The W-30 package for this model year added only $263 to the price.

You would have expected Oldsmobile to advertise the fact that this 1970 442 was a W machine, right? Wrong! The only numbers that appeared on the trunk were "442." The W-30 identification was featured only on the lower front quarters.

This factory photo vividly illustrates the 1968 W-30 engine system. The powerplant featured such full-race goodies as free-flow exhaust, head and distributor modifications, heat-treated valve spring and damper assemblies, aluminum six-blade fan with slip clutch, and cold-air induction air cleaner. **Oldsmobile**

For the first time in 1969, W-30 identification was visible in the form of a decal on the front quarter. A year later it would be a chrome emblem, but just having that W on the machine was enough for most performance enthusiasts.

The 1969 W-30 was available in three 442 models: the convertible, the club coupe, and the hardtop. A total of 1,389 were sold.

The 1970 W-30 used the 455 engine. The W componentry on this awesome powerplant provided an extra 5hp over the standard 455 mill. The engine produced an amazing 500lb-ft of torque.

In 1970, a chrome W-30 medallion was placed directly below the 442 nomenclature, in the full-body side stripe.

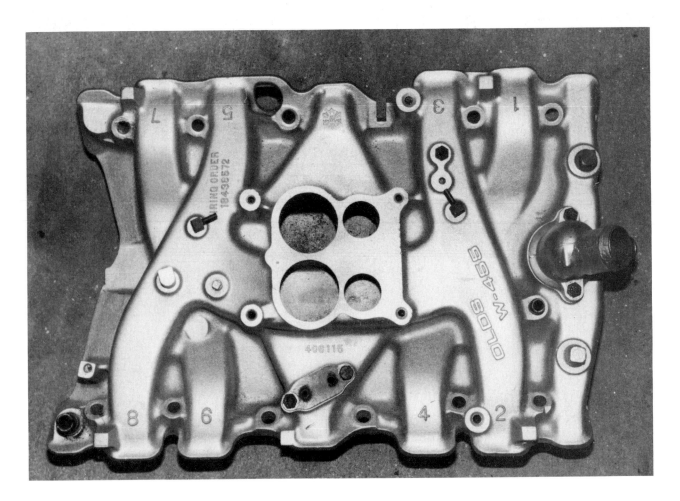

The infamous Dr. Oldsmobile was the main performer in the car maker's advertising of the W machines during the late sixties and early seventies. The legendary ads featured the Doctor and his strange horde of henchmen. **Oldsmobile advertisement**

duction setup bore a marked similarity to that of Ford's factory drag racer, the Thunderbolt.

The dark, elongated scoops in the bumper gave subtle notice to what was under the hood. The system was known as the Force Air induction system. The W-30's stouter valve springs and hotter cam optimized the powerplant for the induction system.

Make no mistake, these first W-30-equipped cars are rare, with only fifty-four produced. The majority were F-85 club coupes. That number probably was higher since a number of dealers installed the W-30 hardware.

The aluminum intake manifold for the 455 W-30 powerplant was an intricate casting, as seen here. Note the unmistakable W-455 imprint.

If you can prove that you've got a factory setup, obviously it's a more valuable acquisition. But either way, it's a collectible–an extremely rare and powerful Oldsmobile.

The initial W-30 equipment could be added to any powerplant as a dealer-installed kit and a few of the tri-carbed L-69s were equipped with the W-30 package. The W-30-equipped L-69 was rated at 360hp, the same as the standard L-69, but you know those W-30 goodies were worth a number of additional ponies!

Racing was the easy way to prove a performance point in those days, and the drag strip performance of the Olds L-69 W-30 didn't disappoint the boys in the boardroom. A W-30 L-69 won the National Hot Rod Association's C-Stock title. Those were impressive results for the first time out.

Olds didn't announce the W-30 option on the car, but it happened. So, only performance nuts

The 1971 W-30 wasn't quite what it had been in past years. Performance was sapped by lower compression ratios, and in the minds of many, the machine's brutish looks had also been toned down. But the W-30 still got the attention of those who wanted performance.

could identify the potent W-30-equipped machines. The only exterior clue was the subtle air scoops in the front bumper. That, however, would change in the years to come.

1967 W-30

One would have thought that the high exposure the W-30 option was accorded during its first year would have caused Olds big wigs to more vigorously announce its presence, but again, that was not the case for 1967.

For the W-30's second year, the 400ci mill featured a Rochester four-barrel.

The second year W-30 was an upgraded package available as a dealer-installed option that featured some "full-race" modifications. The Force Air induction system was modified to accommodate the new front-end. The headlights for the 1967 442 were separated with the parking light mounted in the middle, with four induction scoops spaced above and below each

The twin humps on the 1971 W-30 hood spoke of performance and power. Olds enthusiasts consider this design to be one of the best of the breed.

The new powerplant ground rules called for 8.5:1 compression ratios, but the machine still looked its old performance self.

parking lamp. The left side tubing took up the space reserved for the battery, which moved to the trunk, as in a pure-bred drag car.

Besides the monstrous ram air tubes, another aspect of the W-30 engine compartment caught your eye. Olds engineers trimmed weight by using bright red fiberglass inner fenders. Very un-factory-like, and very hard to miss when the hood was lifted.

Other changes included a new capacitive discharge ignition system and a hotter cam with a longer 308 degree duration. The second-year W-30 package produced a real performer on the strip, occasionally turning sub-fourteen-second quarter mile times.

Again, the trick powerplant was not touted outside the engine compartment, and wouldn't be until decals indicated W packages on the 1969 models. Although the model fell in line with the public's appetite for muscle, only 502 W packages were sold,

The hood stripes for the 1971 442, and also the W-30 version, were identical to those of the previous year. They remained popular with the buying public—at least those who were still into performance.

These hood hold-downs had also been available on the 1970 W-30. Their presence testified to the type of performance available from these machines.

The slotted design of the Super Stock II wheels was popular during the W years. This style was available on the 1971 W-30.

making the W-30-equipped 1967s one of the rarest Olds muscle cars.

1968 W-30

The restyled and rakish A-body design complemented the power image of the W-30 option for 1968. And for the first time, Olds acknowledged the W-30 in company literature, and hinted at the magic of the moniker.

Olds literature warned potential buyers about the rough idle characteristics of the W-30 powerplant, and that it might not be applicable for all. But 1,911 performance-oriented buyers were willing to take that chance. And you can bet most of them wish they had the car today!

The large grill induction ducts were gone from the bumper of the 1968 W-30 and now were located directly below. The air cleaner changed to a twin-snorkel version of the standard Olds cleaner. Horsepower was still a sizzling 360, 35hp over the standard 442 powerplant.

The W-30 package was priced at $263. Engine modifications included the ram air system, a 328 degree cam, and stiffer valve springs. It was about as good a powerplant as you could get with a factory label, and the engine was meticulously prepared.

That price was extremely cheap and the package included either the M-40 automatic or M-21 four-speed transmission, heavy-duty radiator, and high-performance rear-end componentry.

Once again, there was no identification externally, so a number of W experts have been able to acquire these machines for bargain prices. It's difficult to comprehend why, in the midst of the muscle era, the W wasn't shown for all to see. Why have that kind of performance under the hood if most of the buying public didn't know about it?

Finally, here's an interesting bit of trivia about the 1968 W-30. There wasn't adequate vacuum pressure for the power brakes because of the radical cam design. Hence, there were no power brakes on these haulers. But the folks that bought these models weren't looking for creature comforts, right?

1969 W-30

The performance magic of the W-30 kept right on going for 1969. For the first year, it was available only on 442 models. The slotted ducts below the redesigned grill still betrayed the W-30 under the hood, but *finally* the buyer no longer had to search the front end to see if it was indeed a W muscle machine. W-30 decals were affixed on the front corners just above the marker lights. It was nice, but it seemed that the W-30 deserved more than just a sticker.

Oldsmobile sales literature for 1969 spoke boldly of the W-30 option: "W-30 means Force Air induction with mammoth front air scoops; wide -hroat dual air ducts; dual-intake air cleaner; minimum combustion chamber volume; separated center exhaust ports for optimum timing; big intake and exhaust valves; streamlined and individually-branched exhaust manifold; high-overlap cam; low-restriction dual exhaust; and a pair of whopper hood paint patches."

The company took special care in assembling these potent powerplants. Tolerances were extremely tight, as was also the case with the heavy-duty underpinnings. The limited-slip rear ends were available with a stump-pulling 4.66:1 ratio.

Even though the exhaust ports and cylinder heads were changed, horsepower was still listed at 360. Torque was rated at 440lb-ft at 3600rpm.

In 1969 Oldsmobile ads first used Dr. Olds—a devious-looking character who performed magic with performance elixirs. Always garbed in a white lab coat, sporting a handlebar mustache, and accompanied by his seedy-looking band of assistants, the small performance army promoted various W modifications. The good doctor became an institution whose mystique remains, even into the nineties.

W-30 production for 1969 was down somewhat with only 1,389 sold. With numbers like that, it's easy to understand why these cars are rare today. Potential buyers should make sure they are getting the real thing, perhaps by consulting with an Olds expert before making a purchase.

An interesting aside is that the 1968 and 1969 W-30 400ci engines carried 455 engine rods and cranks. The bore was reduced 0.105 inches to maintain 400ci of displacement.

The slotted wheel design for the 1974 W-30 carried a beauty ring. The reflection of the slots in the ring gave the wheel a unique look that is still in style in the nineties.

1970 W-30

Entering the first year of the new decade, the 442 line got the 455ci engine (rated at 365 hp) under the hood, as did the W-30. Again, the W-30 components rated five extra horsepower (370hp at 5200rpm), a conservative amount to be sure. The trademark in-

The large W-30 numbers appeared again in 1979, but they signified cosmetics rather than performance.

There weren't any markings on the exterior of the 1968 Cutlass or F-85, except for the Ram Rod 350, to show their W-31 lineage. It wasn't until the following year that the model would display the W-31 name.

duction tubes were gone, but the twin-scoop W-25 fiberglass induction hood remained. The functional arrangement featured a solid connection that funneled cooler outside air directly into the Rochester four-barrel carb.

The brand-new 455 featured hydraulic lifters, five main bearings, and dual exhaust. It was not surprising that the torque was rated at an amazing 500lb-ft at only 3600rpm. The impressive performance numbers were required because the 1970 W-30 weighed in at almost 3,700 pounds. Even so, a *Car Life* magazine

The first W-31 was known as the Ram Rod 350. Model ID was a decal depicting two pistons and a crank.

66

The W-31 was only one numeral higher than its big-block brother the W-30. This boiling small-block, though, was nothing to scoff at with 325 pounding horses. This 1969 model was tested at 14.5 seconds in the quarter.

road test showed a 14.36 second run for the quarter mile. Very impressive, indeed!

The compression ratio still stood at a healthy 10.5:1 and the engine carried an aluminum intake manifold. The cam, though, was slightly milder than the radical 328 degrees of the previous year.

Surprisingly, a majority of the minimal production figure carried automatics as opposed to four-speeds, the expected transmission for a performance machine.

The 1970 W-30 suspension was up to the task withheavy-duty coil springs, Delco telescopic shocks, and 0.937 inch front and 0.875 inch rear diameter sway bars.

Eye-catching fiberglass inner fenders were still a part of the W-30 package, along with front disc brakes. New to the model was a W-30 chrome badge on the front quarters just below the 442 numbers, and in the midst of the body-length stripe.

The 1970 W-30 is the ultimate of the W modifications, in the minds of most collectors. The downturn would start the following year, and this kind of big-block performance would never return.

One of the best of this breed is the beautifully restored machine of Bill Streeter. This prize winner is loaded to the hilt with just about every available option.

Streeter restored the car himself, and his craftsmanship is flawless. He also turned quarter mile times of 13.88 seconds at 100mph on street-legal tires.

One of the interesting options this W-30 carries is the W-27 aluminum rear end cover which saved twenty-two pounds. Streeter says that option was available only on the W cars of the era.

An interesting footnote was a March 1970 article in *Car Life,* where they road tested a so-called W-30 station wagon, a one-of-a-kind Vista Cruiser equipped with a W-30 powertrain. It was one hot hauler, but its whereabouts are unknown.

1971 W-30

Performance started going down the tubes in 1971, and, unfortunately, the W-30 also faltered a bit. The two-point compression ratio drop that hit other members of the Olds engine family also degraded the W-30 455 to 300hp, a monumental drop of seventy horses. It was a sign of the times. The showroom felt the effects of the decreasing interest in performance, with only 920 W-30s built–810 hardtop coupes and 110 convertibles.The new ground rules for the once-mighty package included 8.5:1 compression ratio, emissions equipment, and the most damaging, unleaded, low-octane fuel in the tank. The 328 degree cam, however, was still available from the dealer with the four-speed tranny, and surprisingly, performance wasn't down that much.

Word was that with a good driver at the wheel, high fourteen-second performance was still possible with the help of the double-disc clutch option. Torque was still extremely impressive with the W-30 powerplant pounding out 410lb-ft of torque. No doubt about it, the chrome W-30 side markings were still deserved.

For muscle enthusiasts, the 1971 W-30 is considered to be just a touch off the 1970 model, but with its dynamite looks, handling, and only slightly degraded performance, this is still a valuable collectible.

1972 W-30

For 1972, the W-30 was shamelessly downgraded to an optional feature of the 442 package. The 442 slipped back to an optional addition to the Cutlass, and the W-30 package received a demotion as well.

The W-30 option package (which cost the buyer an extra $599) still included the 455 powerplant (albeit downgraded) hooked up with a four-barrel. It was listed at 300hp net, and still featured the forced air fiberglass hood, heavy-duty radiator, and dual exhaust. The only available rear-end ratio was 3.42.

The W-30 identification remained directly below the 442 emblem, and the model had a special paint job. Perhaps the designers found it difficult to let the W-30 die, so this model looked the part even though the powertrain's energy had been drained. In fact, 442 and W-30 ads concentrated on handling rather than performance.

Richard Potter owns a top-notch example of a 1972 W-30. The Viking Blue beauty has been in his possession since 1979, and the restoration process has been continuous. Total authenticity was his goal.

Consider the distinctive body-length stripe. That's no decal. "With help from my brother, we used original blueprints and painted it on. That's the way it was, and the way I wanted it," Potter explains.

The option sheets indicated that the red fiberglass inner panels were no longer available for this model year, but Potter's machine has them. "The dealer and original owner said they were there when the car arrived from the factory, and they're staying in place," he says.

The classy W-30 was one of only 289 equipped with a four-speed. Not surprisingly, the car won its class at the 1991 Oldsmobile Club of America Nationals.

1973 and Later W-30s

For 1973, the famous W number vanished completely. Performance cars and long gas lines don't exactly go together. Even the 442, which was around in name only, was only an appearance package with wimpy power under the hood. For performance this model year, it was necessary to look for a used W-30.

Needless to say, they were available for bargain prices. Nobody wanted a gas-gulping big-block in those days, not to mention a high-performance version. Sadly, the performance era was over.

The W-30 nomenclature appeared a number of times during the seventies on the Hurst/Olds models and on the 1980 Cutlass Calais hardtop coupe. Again, the emblem had nothing to do with performance— just remembrances of the good old days. By the way, there were 886 sold.

But there are two other W machines of that wonderful era to discuss, the W-31 and the W-32.

The W-31 Option

The W-30–equipped 400ci and 455ci mills were the top guns of the Olds performance line, but there was another muscle movement that caught the fancy of many. Those big-blocks were beyond the financial reach of many. Oldsmobile's answer was to soup–up small-block powerplants with the same componentry that made the W-30 great. The 400ci version was the W-32, while the 350ci unit was eventually named the W-31.

1968 W-31

The Ram Rod 350 was the name given to the first W-31, even though it was never designated a W car. The Ram Rod was identified with a fender–mounted decal depicting the end view of two pistons, rods, and a crank with the words Ram Rod 350. The W-31

Was this a great-looking muscle car, or what? This small-block W-31, the 1969 version, carried an ID decal on the front quarter (just above the marker light).

nomenclature was nowhere to be found.

Even though the 442 model carried the Olds performance image, the W-31 package was not used in a 442 during the three years of W-31 production. Without the expected 442 designation on the flanks, the unsuspecting might have been convinced the W-31 was just another Cutlass. Not!

The W-31 option was popular with the youth market, with 742 sold that first model year. The package was available with the F-85 club coupe (36 sold), the Cutlass Supreme coupe (30 sold), and the Cutlass base model which attracted 674 buyers.

A W-31 would be a significant find, but rest assured, not an easy accomplishment. The W-30's Force Air induction system appeared on the W-31, with Ram Rod 350 decals on the twin-snorkel air cleaner. When combined with two-inch intake heads, a potent W-30 style cam, and a four-barrel Rochester carb, the engine pumped out an impressive 320hp.

The year 1969 was the second year the W-31 option package was produced, but it was the first year the package would be called the W-31. Model ID was displayed on the front quarter, a decal above the side marker light.

The second-year W-31 came with lots of performance good-ies in addition to a boiling Ram Rod 350 mill. The package included a special suspension, close-ratio four-speed trans-mission, limited-slip rear axle, and forced air induction (note the air intake scoop under the bumper).

It was strictly manual gear changing for the W-31, with both the M-20 and M-21 four-speeds and the M-14 three-speed available. Although no figures are available, one can bet that the four-speeds were the more popular choice.

Dean Picaro of Springfield, Ohio, owns a beautiful 1968 W-31 (Ram Rod 350). Picaro bought the car for only $500. Needless to say, he spent considerably more bringing it to its present condition. He'll tell you that even though there is only a small-block under the hood, the performance is excellent. The car has turned high-fourteen second quarter mile times with Picaro behind the wheel.

The first W-31 fared impressively on the nation's drag strips, and its performance was considered un-derrated by many experts.

1969 W-31

For the W-31 option's second year, changes were minimal and production was up slightly to 931 units. About midyear, a W-31 convertible could be ac-quired, although only twenty-six sold.

Olds advertised the 1969 W-31 as "Having it your way with available goodies as long as your arm; 4 speeds with close-or-wide ratio, anti-spin axle, tach, wide-boot blackwalls with raised white letters, Super Stock wheels, and on and on."

A March 1969 *Car and Driver* road test showed the W-31 to be right with the competition in the quarter, with 14.5 second capabilities in place. Top speed was listed at 132mph. The air induction system was refined by adding vacuum valves which intro-

The final year for the W-31 was 1970, and the small-block hauler was a significant performer. The characteristic induc-tion tubes were replaced by hood scoops that took air di-rectly into the top of the air cleaner. Horsepower was adver-tised at 325, the same as the standard 442 powerplant, even though the W-31 mill was sporting an aluminum in-take manifold.

duced engine-compartment air into the Quadrajet four-barrel during warm-up. Horsepower was listed at 325. *Car and Driver* noted that the W-31 was a machine for the performance advocate. "You have to feather the clutch to get launched, and once underway, it chugs and bucks when you try to idle along in gear...But when the needle reaches four digits, the problems are over. Everything goes quiet–the lull before the storm."

A handling package could be added to the W-31 to complement its formidable straight-line performance. A front suspension bar, heavy-duty shocks, and F70x14 wide-oval rubber were available.

Power brakes were *not* available on the 1969 W-31 (also true for the 1968) for the same reason power brakes were omitted from the W-30: insufficient vacuum pressure due to the high-profile cam. Again, the W-31 was identified by only a decal on the front quarters.

1970 W-31

The final W-31 was a dynamic looker with a re-designed fiberglass ram air hood, body-length stripe, and chrome W-31 badges. One might assume this great–looking muscle car is a 442—a logical mis-

Considering the performance mindset of the era, you would have thought that Oldsmobile would have prominently announced the W-31 option. They didn't–the rear end of the car was clean as a whistle. A decal on the front quarter was all that indicated the power under the hood.

In its second and final year, the W-31 was identified by a chrome emblem embedded within the full body-length stripe. The model also boasted a new fiberglass ram air hood that was completely functional.

take—but it's a W-31 Cutlass.

The major change for the 1970 W-31 was the deletion of the long induction tubes. The outside air now came through the hood scoops and directly into the air cleaner. The system's effectiveness was increased due to the positive connection seal on the top of the air cleaner.

Horsepower was reported at 325 at 5400rpm, even though the mill featured a new aluminum intake manifold. The powerplant carried good innards with a 0.474 inch lift and 308 degree duration cam, 2.005 inch intake and 1.630 inch exhaust valves, medium-rate valve springs, hydraulic lifters, and flat-top racing pistons. The W-31 was a factory street car with all the makings of a late-model stock car.

Again, there was inadequate vacuum pressure to

Where long induction tubes had previously pulled the outside air from the grill area, the 1970 W-31 used an induction-style hood to perform the same function. There was a positive connection between the hood and the top of the air cleaner.

The 1970 W-31 could prove to be a desirable muscle collectible during the nineties. Although not carrying a big-block, the high-performance 350 powerplant stood tall on both street and strip.

operate power brakes. The new manual front disc brakes helped the situation.

It was still a solid fourteen-second quarter-mile performer, even with the Turbo Hydra-matic transmission. The standard rear end was the 3.91 geared limited-slip unit.

When Dan Hill acquired his W-31, he really didn't know what he had. "I was looking for a '70 Cutlass, but this was available so I bought it just for transportation," Hill explains. He later discovered the car was a W-31, and restored it.

When younger car enthusiasts view this magnificent orange hauler, they find it hard to believe that such a street machine could have emerged from the factory. Dan assures us, though, that this is exactly the way it was on the showroom floor!

The last W-31 was the best-selling with 1,352 sold, the Cutlass hardtop being by far the most popular (1,029 sold).

So with that upward turn, why no 1971 W-31? Well, as any performance enthusiast of the time would tell you, it was the beginning of the end as far as big power was concerned, and the W-31 was one of the first casualties. From a collector's viewpoint, these machines don't rate the same interest or value as the W-30s, but one of these low production W machines would be worth the effort to restore. It was truly the best of Olds small-block muscle.

The W-32 Option

We're not quite finished with the W story yet. There was one more W designation, the W-32 option package, which was a combination of the 442 and an upgraded 400ci powerplant. The W-32 lasted for only two years (1969 and 1970) and is often forgotten. It definitely deserved better!

1969 W-32

The only identification on the 1969 W-32 was W-32 decals located directly above the front quarter marker lights. The model was introduced midyear as an option available with the 442 only.

The 350hp 400ci mill was the player here, which used a more civil 286 degree, 0.472 inch of lift, and 58 degree overlap cam. The Force Air system with the

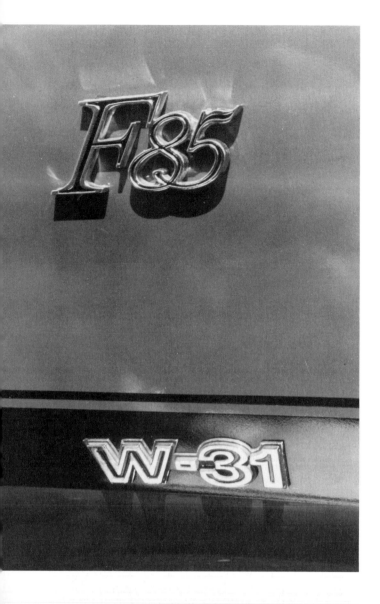

under-bumper scoops was again in place for this rare W machine, but the W-32 was available only with the Turbo Hydra-matic 400 automatic transmission. Separated center exhaust ports and individually branched exhaust manifolds were also a part of these gutsy mills.

The suggested retail price for the W-32 option was $121.12, and it carried the nomenclature of Force-Air Street Engine. The W-32 package, which was available with all three 442 bodystyles, included anti-spin rear axle, heavy-duty radiator, and W-style hood stripes. The model also carried under-bumper air scoops, but the inner fenderwells were black instead of the red fiberglass of the W-30 and W-31. Oddly, only the beefed-up powerplant is listed on the W-32 slip. By the way, a fully decked-out W-32 could be procured for the price of about $3,300! What a buy!

Reportedly, only 297 of this rare W model were constructed. Undoubtedly, many have lost their W-32 identification with repaints covering the W-32 decals forever.

Rick Blowers owns one of the oft–forgotten W-32s and he's impressed with its performance. "The Turbo 400 was specially modified with the W-32 with firmer shifts, higher stall converter, and higher shift points," Blower comments. To best characterize this first W-32, Blower says, would be to call it a streetable version of the W-30.

Steve Hunkins also has one of those rare W-32s, a machine found sitting forelornly on a used car lot in 1978. "I really wasn't in the market for a project at the time, but I knew what these machines were, and I just couldn't pass it up," Hunkins explains.

In addition to the rare W-32 designation, Hunkins' W-32 is a convertible. What more could you ask for?

1970 W-32

A very small number of W-32 machines were built in 1970. The 442 no longer received the option, however. That honor went to the Cutlass Supreme, which also carried the SX package (to be discussed in Chapter 6).

A 455ci engine with 365hp available made the W-32 great in its second year. Once again, the stan-

The final year for the W-31 was 1970. Too bad, because this small-block hauler was cheaper to insure than the big-block muscle machines. And check out those dynamite looks!

The 1970 442's functional hood scoops were doing their thing with the W-31 option. The W-31 replaced the 442's big-block with a high-performance small-block 350 mill.

dard transmission was the M-40 Turbo Hydra-matic. Also this year, the W-32 included dual exhaust, but the decals were gone. When you get right down to it, all the W-32 consisted of in its second and final year was an engine option. In fact, you'd really have to call it an "unofficial W-32."

The W Option Into the Nineties

The W designation appeared on various Oldsmobile models through the seventies, but it just wasn't the same. In 1970, for example, Olds offered a W-33 455ci/390hp performance package option for the heavyweight Delta 88 model. That same year, a W-34

The rocket emblem appeared here and there decades after its introduction. Here it is on the trunk lock of a 1970 Cutlass W-31.

Despite the W-31's racy looks and heavy performance, it never received the recognition it deserved. The W-3l did, however, receive a chrome emblem.

option included a 455ci/400hp Rocket powerplant, and was available on the luxury Toronado.

Again, remember that the little-used W-29 designation (which designated the 442) was around through the 1979 model. There was also a W-42 option from 1985 through 1987, an appearance option for various Cutlass coupes, which managed to sell over 4,200 the final two years it was available.

"W" meant a little more performance when it was used with the Quad 4 high-revving powerplant. In 1990, the W-40 stood for the Quad 4 Sport Performance Package, and Olds sold 2,629. For old-time Olds performance fans, it was good to see the "W" on something with a little punch.

In 1991, a Calais S W-40 sport model attracted 1,364 buyers. The following year, the Calais S was offered with a W-41 option. Even though it was only a four-cylinder, it was a sign that performance was coming back.

But it was the famous W-30, and to a lesser extent the W-3l and W-32, that will always be remem-

bered and savored. It was an era of factory performance that may never be matched.

W-30 Production

Year	Bodystyle	Production
1966	F-85 club coupe	25
	F-85 hardtop	8
	Cutlass coupe	5
	Cutlass hardtop	<u>16</u>
		54
1967	Cutlass Supreme hardtop coupe	363
	Cutlass club coupe	<u>129</u>
		492
1968	442 convertible	170
	442 club coupe	315
	442 hardtop	<u>1,426</u>
		1,911
1969	442 convertible	121
	442 club coupe	171

W-30 Production

Year	Bodystyle	Production
	442 hardtop	<u>1,097</u>
		1,389
1970	442 convertible	264
	442 club coupe	262
	442 hardtop coupe	<u>2,574</u>
		3,100
1971	442 convertible	110
	442 hardtop coupe	<u>810</u>
		920
1972	Cutlass hardtop coupe	17
	Cutlass club coupe	19
	Cutlass hardtop coupe	623
	Cutlass Supreme convertible	<u>113</u>
		772

W-31 Production

Year	Bodystyle	Production
1968	Cutlass Supreme coupe	30
	Cutlass	674
	F-85 club coupe	<u>38</u>
		742
1969	Cutlass hardtop coupe	569
	Cutlass club coupe	106
	Cutlass convertible	26
	F-85 club coupe	<u>212</u>
		913
1970	F-85 club coupe	207
	Cutlass club coupe	116
	Cutlass hardtop coupe	<u>1,029</u>
		1,352

W-32 Production

Year	Bodystyle	Production
1969	442 hardtop	247
	442 convertible	25
	442 sedan	<u>25</u>
		297
1970	unknown	unknown

The "Ram Rod" designation was still in place on the air cleaner of this 1969 W-32 powerplant. The 400ci power-plant was capable of mid-fourteen-second dashes down the drag strip. The twin-snorkel air cleaner induction system helped boost horsepower to 325.

W Option Powerplants

Year	Cubic Inches	Hp @ rpm	Production
1966	400	360 @ 5000	(W-30) 54
1967	400	360 @ 5400	(W-30) 502
(Dealer-installed option)			
1968	400	360 @ 5400	(W-30) 1,911
	350	320 @ 5400	(W-31) 742
1969	400	360 @ 5400	(W-30) 1,389
	400	350 @ 5200	(W-32) 297
	350	325 @ 5400	(W-31) 913
1970	455	370 @ 5400	(W-30) 1,300
	350	325 @ 5400	(W-31) 1,352
			(W-32) unknown
1971	455	350bhp/300nhp	(W-30) 920
1972	455	300nhp @ 4700	(W-30) 772

A 400ci mill was used in the late sixties to early seventies W cars and, in this case, on the little-known W-32. The model was built in 1969 and 1970. This 1969 version is one of only 297 built that year.

The W-32 was manufactured for two years and employed a 400ci powerplant. It never received a chrome W-32 emblem.

The immaculate W-32 owned by Rick Blowers. It is one of the best of the breed in the nation. **Rick Blowers.**

Chapter 4

The Hurst/Olds

Mention the name Hurst and all kinds of things come to mind: performance, style, class, and beautiful spokesperson Linda Vaughn!

That red and blue block "H" with an oval-encircled "Hurst" below and to the right said it all. And fortunately for the Olds line, the connection between Hurst/Olds and performance was made. What evolved through their association was a series of specially–prepared Hurst/Olds models known for performance boosts and innovative styling.

Six Hurst/Olds were produced during the muscle years, with no particular regularity: 1968, 1969, 1973, 1974, 1975, and 1979. A number were built during the early eighties (1983 and 1984), but the horsepower couldn't qualify the Hurst/Olds as a performance car. Frankly, the Hurst/Olds produced in the eighties were all show and no go.

The muscle-era Hurst was a performance kick-in-the-pants that Olds really needed. The company barely publicized the killer J-2 and L-69 tri-carb setups. That wouldn't be the case with these Hurst machines, though, because of the urging of Olds engineer Doc Watson, the man who inspired "Dr. Olds," the fictional character featured in advertising for the early Hurst models.

1968

The initial Hurst model (H/O for short, not to be confused with another term of the period, HO, which represented High Output) was just the ticket for the Oldsmobile image, and through the years, the initial Hurst/Olds has become one of the most desirable of all the vintage muscle machines. Looking at the model's performance and unique appearance, it's easy to understand its appeal.

The biggest attraction rested under that bawdy black and silver hood. The 455ci big-block was capable of 390hp (gross) at only 5000rpm, and an awe-inspiring 500lb-ft of torque at 3600rpm.

The 455 was unique to the Hurst/Olds in 1968, as the standard 442 was powered by the 400. The standard 442 received the 455 in 1970, and its rating was 25hp less than the 1968 H/O figure. The 390hp

The 1968 Hurst/Olds was a killer street performer, with a 455i mill punching out an impressive 390hp and 500lb-ft of torque. The powerplant employed hydraulic lifters and a 10.25:1 compression ratio.

If you saw this hood design in the next lane, you knew that you were in for one tough challenge. The functional and beautiful hood was one of the defining characteristics of the 1969 Hurst/Olds.

The first-year (1968) Hurst/Olds had a distinct appearance. The overall color was a somewhat dull gun-metal grey, detailed with black striping. The car had a bit of a sinister look.

Hurst mill was by far the most powerful engine offered in 1968, with the standard 400 putting out 350hp and the W-30 bumping up 10 to 360hp.

The powerful Hurst/Olds mill carried the W-30 Force Air induction system, with snorkel tubing, under-grill scoops, a high-lift cam, and special carburetor jetting. In stock trim, it sounded like a Pro Stock dragster. To cool this behemoth mill, Hurst added a high-capacity cooling system with a viscous fan clutch and high-density radiator core. Such a powerful engine merited the additional cooling capacity.

Two powerplants were available with the first Hurst/Olds, both 455ci mills borrowed from the Toronado. The W-45 was a 390hp engine for cars

This view shows a number of the unique features of the 1968 Hurst/Olds. Note the unique black body striping and under-bumper scoop (one of two) that funnels cool outside air into the twin-snorkel air cleaner.

If you liked your Olds muscle machines bright and sporty, you probably wouldn't have liked the 1968 Hurst/Olds. That was just not its style, with the grey base color and black striping.

The Hurst/Olds used the same slotted wheels that could be ordered with other bodystyles. They went well with the first H/O model.

without air conditioning, while the W-46 was for the cool-air versions. Oldsmobile constructed the engines with larger-than-normal tolerances to reduce friction. Both were identified on the twin-snorkel air cleaner cover as "Oldsmobile Rocket 455." Never had that old Rocket name tag stood so tall!

A ton of additional goodies adorned this first H/O to whet the appetite of the performance-minded. The standard Hydra-matic was modified to match the dramatic new powerplant. (Reportedly, one four-speed was built, as well. Anybody out there ever see it?) Topside, a console-mounted Hurst (what else?) dual-gate shifter selected the gears. Also, the heavy-duty rear end included extra-strong axle shafts and gearing.

In a brochure passed out to Hurst buyers, Olds explained how to operate the dual-gate shifter. The

A small packet of information was given to each buyer of the 1968 Hurst/Olds. Included were tips on the machine's operation and "special components." The materials congratulated the buyer as a new member of the "Hurst/Olds Fraternity." Oldsmobile Factory Booklet

There was no mistaking the famous Hurst/Olds dual emblem on the lower front quarter.

Advertised performance of the 1969 455 Hurst/Olds powerplant was 10hp less than the previous year, at 380hp, although it had the same 500lb-ft torque capability.

explanation went like this: "You will notice two separate gates: the one on the left side is for normal automatic operation employing standard detents, reverse inhibitor spring and parking-spring lock: the one on the right is for manual operation; for upshifting." It then went into extreme detail on how to utilize the high-tech shifter. "It's not as complicated at it sounds...one or two passes up and down and you'll be shifting like a pro!" the brochure stated.

Handling was superb, with a rear sway bar and heavy-duty suspension pieces. New front disc brakes, equipped with a proportioning valve, greatly improved stopping efficiency. Slap on the Goodyear G70x14s and stand back!

The performance took your breath away. With the 3.91:1 rear-end ratio (in the non-air conditioned models), high thirteen-second performances were just a quarter-mile away. Add slicks and headers and you could get into the twelves.

There was no mistaking this machine. The

The 1969 Hurst/Olds was a ray of sunshine compared to the initial model. The new model featured bright white with gold detailing. To many, it was the best-looking Hurst machine.

Hurst/Olds identification was carried in the blacked-out grill on both front quarters, the right rear corner of the rear deck, wheel cover centers, and on the glove box door. Ol' Doc Watson even got a credit at that final location.

You'd have to call the base color of the '68 Hurst/Olds gun-metal grey; Olds called it Peruvian Silver and it was richly set off by black detailing. Overall, the car's appearance was somewhat subdued, certainly not screaming what the potent package contained.

The black covered the rear deck with twin hood stripes. Also, a black stripe swept from the rear point of the right side window, across the front door, and to the top of the front fender. By the way, the red fiberglass inner fenders were in place underneath the hood.

Open the doors and you found a combination of

luxury and sports car. The interior was highlighted by a woodgrain wheel and Rocket Rally-Pac gauges and tach. That awesome 455 mill could really swing those dials into action. The interior motif was sinister black with walnut door panels.

The initial Hurst/Olds actually had to be snuck out of the factory. At the time, GM had strict rules that there would be *nothing* bigger than a 400ci power-plant installed in an A-body midsize chassis. To get around this dilemma, Doc Watson simply moved the final production assembly to Demmer Engineering in Lansing, Michigan. The 442s, which served as the basis for this magnificent machine, were moved to the Demmer facility right off the production line. Even with the work done out-of-factory, the Hurst/Olds was still covered by an Olds warranty. It might have been stretching the rules a bit, but it was carried off successfully.

Production of these initial H/Os was minimal due to the late-year release. A total of only 515 were constructed, 459 Holiday hardtops and 56 Sports Coupes. Only about a quarter of the haulers (123 to be exact) carried air conditioning. Obviously, performance was in the forefront of the buyers' minds!

Not surprisingly, the requests for the Hurst/Olds

far exceeded that minimal production run. Olds probably could have sold many times that number had they been available. As the Hurst ads at the time stated, "Seeing is believing...Owning is unreal."

To many performance collectors of the nineties, finding *any* Hurst/Olds is a significant feat, but acquiring this first of the breed is the ultimate accomplishment.

1969

If you liked the 1968 model for its different look, the 1969 Hurst/Olds would have blown you away. Where the first H/O was somewhat drab in grey and black, the 1969 was a gold and white ray of sunshine. It was a knockout!

Olds called the colors Cameo White and Firefrost Gold. The lower portion of the body and two upper racing stripes were gold. In addition, a gold band dissected the twin-scooped hood, along with coating the top of the oh-so-functional scoops. Fifteen-inch wheels carried a chrome outer rim painted argent silver. Finally, there was a broad gold over-roof and rear deck swab that gave the '69 Hurst (Option W-46) a full-race look.

The Hurst identification was plastered on the front quarters, rear deck, and glove box, although, for some reason it was eliminated from the grill. Large H/O 455 decals were on the sides of the rectangular hood scoops. Made no difference, however, as one look told you this was a Hurst. No doubt what was in the other lane if you happened to be engaged in a stop-light confrontation!

The Hurst/Olds' racy design was accentuated by the spoiler fixed to and carried above the rear deck. The unit was functional at speed, reducing aerodynamic drag and pulling laminar airflow off the body. Designers considered making the wing movable so that it would function like an aircraft drag brake, but it ended up being produced in this fixed state.

A spoiler seemed to be required for the muscle look during that era. But the H/O 455's rear appendage was for more than just looks. The spoiler produced about 15psi of downforce at 60mph, and over four times that figure at 120mph.

The awe-inspiring 455 mill was still in place for 1969, but for some reason, Olds downgraded its performance slightly to "only" 380hp. Torque was still 500lb-ft at 3200rpm. The engine was painted red with flashy chrome valve covers. As in 1968, Hurst/Olds models were identified by a "D" cast in front of the left cylinder head and on the rear of the right cylinder head.

The unique air cleaner was completely different from that of the W-30 engine. Instead of the expected ram air hoses, the unit made a closed connection with the underside of the hood. The W-30 would later receive the Hurst-type induction system.

The Hurst/Olds shifted Turbo Hydra-matic was still in place, hooked to a modified three-speed torque converter. The standard ratio for the limited-slip rear

This full-race machine was easily identified as a Hurst/Olds. The name was carried on each side of the prominent hood scoops. H/O badges appeared on the lower front quarters, along with identification on the rear deck and glove box door.

end was 3.42, but a 3.91 unit was also available. A drag test in the March 1969 issue of *Car Life* showed 14.1 second, 100mph quarter-mile performance.

Production was nearly double the previous year, at 906. Except for two convertibles (one of which was given to Hurst cover girl Linda Vaughn), the rest were two-door hardtops. The '69 Hurst/Olds was one of the premier Olds muscle cars–or for that matter, one of the premier muscle cars, period!

Oldsmobile brass wanted this second H/O to be sold a bit differently. One of the model's strong points was that it could bring people into the showroom. And if the salesperson couldn't interest the potential buyer in the H/O, maybe get them interested in one of the other performance models, say the 442.

"Let the Hurst/Olds bring them in," the Olds sales booklet emphasized. "With today's performance market, the Hurst/Olds is the Wildfire. With this model,

you've got the match. The big problem is controlling the flame. As soon as the word is out that you've got a Hurst/Olds...you've got a sizzler in your dealership.

"The youth market (and that's just about everyone these days), will want it...and at any price. So, selling a Hurst/Olds is as easy as falling off a log.

"But that's not the kind of splash that pays off. Strive to get all the 'sales mileage' out of this unique near-one-of-a-kind vehicle as possible."

1970–1971

The 1970 and 1971 model years were big for Oldsmobile with their 442, 1970 Indy pace car, and W machines, but surprisingly, neither model year had a Hurst/Olds model. There was almost a '71 H/O, but the company opted instead for the striking, bright yellow Rallye 350. Nevertheless, the car maker had to know that it had a winner with the Hurst/Olds, and there would be one coming up in 1972.

1972

The crash of the dealer-sponsored Dodge Challenger pace car at the 1971 Indy 500 set the stage for the 1972 Hurst/Olds pacer. The pace car honor was somewhat clouded by that incident, but with the ap-

The 1969 Hurst/Olds carried the Oldsmobile symbol on the rear corner. The rear deck-mounted wing is visible from the side view. Also note the stylish, extremely wide stripe that dissects the rear deck lid.

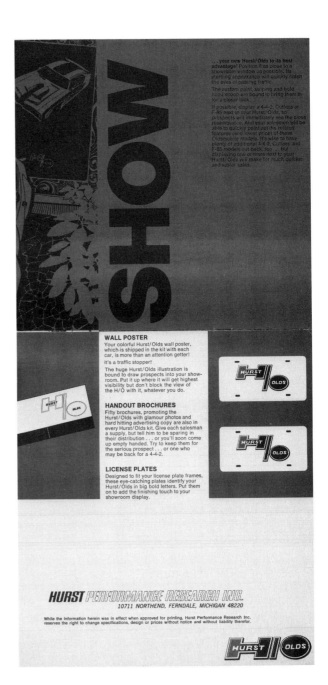

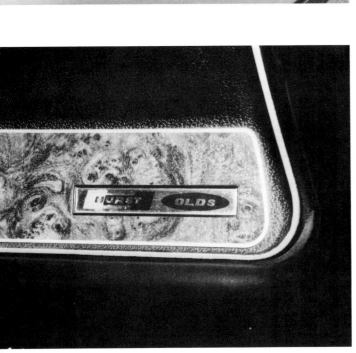

The Hurst/Olds emblem was even carried on the glove box door.

Not only was the 1969 Hurst/Olds new to the buying public, it was also new to the guys in the showroom. This booklet (now rare) instructed salespeople to use the allure of the Hurst/Olds to sell other models. **Oldsmobile Factory Booklet**

There weren't many changes inside the 1969 Hurst/Olds. Production of this second H/O was 906, considerably more than the first year.

pearance of the company-sponsored Hurst/Olds, all was forgotten. For the second time in three years, Olds paced the great race. Production of the H/O pacer replica consisted of 130 convertibles and 499 hardtops, and there certainly was no mistaking these killer machines. The models could be ordered with or without the pace car lettering.

Like the earlier 1969 Hurst, the color scheme was gold and white. The base coat was white with a wide gold band that swept across the lower body, pointed gold strips on the upper front and rear fenders, twin stripes up the rear deck, and a single stripe on the hood. The H/O emblems were carried on the right corner of the rear deck; the badges were located on the lower front quarters on the convertibles, and on the rear top pedestals on the hardtops.

The power to push this Hurst was provided by the W-30 455ci powerplant. The mill was operating at a highly-reduced 8.5:1 compression ratio with a still-impressive net horsepower rating of 300. There

was also a Rallye suspension and certain performance-style suspension pieces. The big-blocks were dropping like flies with other performance models, but hung around for a while on the Hurst models.

1973

A new Cutlass bodystyle meshed nicely with the Hurst/Olds styling and unique detailing for the 1973 model year. The look was completely different this year, with the H/O's traditional white and gold replaced by black with gold trim. The H/O option could be ordered only on the Cutlass S coupe. These machines are extremely hard to find.

The 1973 model featured a broad center hood stripe and a full-length body stripe. The H/O identifying emblems were carried in the middle of the rear opera windows.

The Hurst option was available only with the Cutlass S model for this year, and could be ordered with the 455ci 275nhp powerplant with either the W-45 or W-46 option. The W-45 carried the W-30 springs and valves coupled with a stock 455 cam and a 3.08 rear end.

The W-46 provided more punch with a hotter cam, no air conditioning, and 3.23 gears. The horsepower dropped to 275, but that figure was a net val-

Hurst/Olds designators were on the vinyl roof of the 1972 model, but there wasn't as much power under the hood this year. The model was selected as the 1972 Indy pace car.

The 1972 Hurst/Olds featured the same white and gold color scheme as the earlier 1969 model. Rather than the single center stripe of the 1969 model, the 1972 sported a pair of gold stripes.

The 1972 Hurst/Olds was a bit more subtle than the 1969. The design featured gold striping on the fenders, hood, and rear deck.

ue, and was more impressive than it sounded.

Production of the 1973 Hurst/Olds was the largest yet, with a total of 1,097 coming off the assembly line.

1974

The fifth Hurst/Olds saw dramatic changes under the hood, with the adoption of the 350ci mill (Y-77) as the standard engine. The downturn in performance finally reached even the mighty Hurst. Including the Indy pace car versions, the company listed total production at 1,900.

One small consolation to the performance-minded was the 455 engine option (still carrying a W-30 connotation), but it didn't really deserve the prestigious performance designation with only 250nhp. The dual-gate-shifted Turbo Hydra-Matic 400 tranny and Rallye Suspension required extra cash on the barrelhead.

Again, the model was based on the Cutlass S, and again, the Hurst/Olds would be honored as the Indy pace car. Olds pace cars were becoming a habit, alternating years since 1970.

The styling of this Hurst set it off in a big way. The hood featured the characteristic gold stripe with flat-black hood louvers where the stripe originated. The 15x7 inch Super Stock wheels carried the optional Hurst Loc/Lugs security system. Much attention was given to the rear window, with a modified rear quarter window and a recessed Hurst/Olds exterior emblem. The padded vinyl top had a simulated roll-bar insert.

Other touches included dual color-keyed sport mirrors, optional Hurst molded splash guards, and the optional W-30 engine identification featured on the front quarters. The W-30 package included the Rallye Suspension, dual-snorkel air cleaner, sport steering wheel, heavy-duty cooling, sport console, Turbo Hydra-matic 400, power front disc brakes, instrumentation gauge package, and high-energy ignition.

An optional Indy 500 decal kit was available if you *really* wanted to dress up your Hurst.

1975

The final Hurst/Olds discussed in this book is the 1975 model, which proved to be a much better seller than the previous year, with 2,535 built. This H/O

The good Doc's hand is evident in the striking profile of the 1972 Hurst/Olds.

1974 Hurst/Olds Official Pace Car

Fully Padded Vinyl Top
with Contrasting Simulated
Roll Bar Insert

Modified
Rear Quarter Window

Recessed
Hurst/Olds
Exterior
Emblem

Flat Black Hood Louvers

Hurst Gold
Body Striping

15 x 7 Super
Stock III Wheels

H70 x 15 Raised White
Letter Wide Oval Tires

W-30

Dual Color
Keyed Sport Mirrors

W-30 Engine
Identification

Optional Hurst
Molded Splash Guards

Optional
Hurst Loc/Lugs

1974
with

A unique view of the 1974 Hurst/Olds, as it appeared in this company sales brochure. As many as 1,900 models were sold, over 800 more than the previous year. **Oldsmobile**

modification was available on the Cutlass Supreme hardtop coupe. The classy hauler could be ordered in either black or white, both with the stylish gold striping. Combined with the gold-accented Super Stock III wheels, this was a striking machine.

The 1975 Hurst/Olds was known as the W-25 or W-30, the former carrying the 350ci powerplant, and the long-standing W-30 designation powered by the still–available 455ci powerplant.

The W numbers were blocked out in large decals on the rear of the front quarters. But did the 350 powerplant really *deserve* the "W" designation with only 185nhp? Things were definitely changing when it came to defining performance in the mid-seventies.

One nifty innovation, which came from the 1974 Indy pace car (and which the 1975 model would retain), was a T-top. Safety glass panels could be easily removed to expose the clear blue sky. The vinyl-padded roof panels carried the famous H/O emblem, as did the right-rear corner of the rear deck.

The standard rear-end ratio was 2.56, lower than

additional W-30* features

Rallye Suspension
Dual Snorkel Air Cleaner
Custom Sport Steering Wheel
Heavy Duty Cooling
Sport Console
Performance Turbo Hydramatic
400 Transmission
Power Front Disc Brakes
Instrumentation Gauge Package
High Energy Ignition

*Not available in California.
Y-77 (350 c.i.) appearance package
standard in California and also
available in all cars.

expected for performance. The optional 2.77 or 3.08 ratios helped acceleration somewhat.

1977

In late 1976, a 403ci powered Cutlass S was sent to the Hurst shops for possible conversion. A one-of-a-kind prototype was produced, but that was as far as it went.

Hurst built up that powerplant for increased performance with a marine engine camshaft, stiffer valve springs, a marine-style ignition system, and dual exhaust. A 3.73 rear end helped put the power to the ground. The suspension was modified in "good old days" style with front and rear sway bars and heavy-duty shocks.

The appearance of this 1977 prototype was significantly different from other H/Os. The grill sported a mesh-style screen. The H/O designation was carried on the right rear of the small rear deck spoiler. A long, wide body stripe encompassed both the front and rear marker lights. The fender carried the expected W-30 nomenclature, while "Hurst/Olds" was blocked out within the stripes.

The colors of the proposed 1977 model had not been determined, but it's likely that it would have been either black and gold, or white and gold, the two combinations that had become a tradition with this illustrious model. The lone prototype was black and gold.

It still exists today, in the possession of a private owner.

1979

The last Hurst/Olds of the decade was produced in 1979. It was difficult to call this car a muscle car. It didn't even *look* like one.

The standard powerplant was weak when compared to its brethren. A net horsepower of 170 was all that was available from its 350ci powerplant. The Turbo Hydra-Matic was the standard transmission, with a 2.73 geared rear end. There were a number of appearance items offered, such as special lettering and

One of the best angles from which to view the 1972 Hurst/Olds is from the rear quarter. Note that the H/O emblem was actually carried in the rear deck striping. The machine radiated race car looks and performance!

Although no 1977 Hurst/Olds models made it to the show-room, this prototype was built. **Buick, Oldsmobile, Pontiac Collectors Guide Magazine**

stripes, a Hurst shifter, bucket seats, and a special handling package. So, the 1979 H/O might have *looked* like a performance machine, but that's as far as it went.

Graphics were subdued, with large W-30 decals on the front quarters and the Hurst/Olds emblems on the top pillars. Production, however, was up to 2,529 models. Those buyers didn't purchase the car for its performance, which was a sign of the times.

1983

Once again, the Hurst/Olds went through a dry spell, with no Hurst/Olds produced from 1980 to 1982. Then, in 1983, although it may have been an era of reduced performance, the new Hurst/Olds looked pure performance. The '83 H/O reverted to the black and grey colors of the 1968 model. The black upper body was separated from the lower grey

The one-of-a-kind 1977 Hurst/Olds prototype used a modi-fied 403ci powerplant and a Cutlass S bodystyle. **Buick, Oldsmobile, Pontiac Collectors Guide Magazine**

body by a red stripe. The Hurst/Olds lettering (in red again) was carried on the front quarter and on the lower right corner of the trunk lid.

The powerplant, although not even close to approaching its former glory, was impressive for the time. The 307ci (five-liter) mill produced 180bhp at 4000rpm and 245lb-ft of torque. Not bad performance when you consider that the engine had an 8.0:1 compression ratio.

The engine also featured a low-restriction exhaust system, improved camshaft timing and valvetrain components, and a new engine computer system.

One of the special features of the model was the Hurst Lightning Rods Automatic Shifter. The multiple-stick format provided precise gear changes for both upshifts and downshifts.

Hurst/Olds Production

Year	Bodystyle	Production
1968	442 Hardtop	459
	442 Sports Coupe	56
Total		515
1969	442 Hardtop	904
	442 Convertible	2
Total		906
1970		None produced
1971		None produced
1972	Cutlass Supreme Hardtop	499
	Cutlass Supreme Convertible	130
Total		629
1973	Cutlass	1,097
1974	Cutlass	1,900
1975	Cutlass	2,535
1976		None produced
1977	Cutlass	1 prototype
1978		None produced
1979	Cutlass	2,499
1980		None produced
1981		None produced
1982		None produced
1983	Cutlass	Unknown

You'll note that the graphics for this prototype differed from previous H/Os. Red detailing on the outside of the gold striping made a sharp combination. There is no doubt that this could have been a popular machine. Buick, Oldsmobile, Pontiac Collectors Guide Magazine

It would be difficult to call the 1979 Hurst/Olds a muscle car—the standard 350ci powerplant produced a menial 170nhp.

Chapter 5

Olds Muscle at the Brickyard: Indy Pace Cars

It's always been an honor to be selected to produce the pace car for the "Greatest Spectacle in Racing," otherwise known as the Indy 500.

During the muscle years, Oldsmobiles' association with Indy's aura of speed and power provided great advertising exposure, and the car maker made the most of it.

Olds had the Indy honor twice during the muscle era (1970 and 1972), and then two other times just following the muscle era. Their participation in 1970 was the first time Olds provided the pacer since 1960.

Oldsmobile also paced the great race in 1949, using the brand-new high-compression Rocket powerplant. The actual pacer carried a modified engine that truly could be called a rocket, and set the pattern for the muscle powerplants that would follow.

The V-8 engine installed in the '49 pacer had a 303.7ci displacement and the horsepower greatly exceeded that of previous inline powerplants.

The 1949 pace car didn't look much different than the stock model, with two exceptions. Naturally, the pacer was lettered with the appropriate Indy identification. The other addition was a gigantic chrome rocket that stretched the length of the front fender. Olds engineers initially planned to have the rocket smoking, but that idea was discarded.

The Indy honor was right in line with the performance image that Olds was developing in NASCAR stock car racing.

1970

The 1970 pacer—based on the 442—was officially announced by Oldsmobile on March 2, 1970. The accompanying press release described the upcoming pace car, of which the car maker was justifiably proud. Here's what the release said:

"Oldsmobile is greatly honored to have the 442 chosen as the 1970 pace car. Since being introduced six years ago, the 442 has gained wide acclaim for its

With Oldsmobile receiving acclaim for its powerful engines, it was only fitting that the car maker be honored as the provider of the Indy pace car. The car didn't look that much different from the standard model, except for the expected lettering and the huge rocket adorning the front quarters. **Oldsmobile**

A horde of 1977 pace car replicas line the famed track at Indianapolis. The real pace car holds the honor position in front, carrying the flags on its rear flank. **Indianapolis Motor Speedway**

Eleven years later, another Brickyard honor came Oldsmobile's way with this dazzling 88 convertible. Even though the car that paced the race was heavily modified, the street versions were plenty capable. **Oldsmobile**

styling, performance and handling. Its forthcoming role as pace car for this year's Indy 500 is further testimony to the car's reputation and to Oldsmobile's long tradition for automotive leadership.

"The 442 pace car will be a pearl white convertible with white top and jet black interior trim. Unique black and red striping lend emphasis to the hood, deck lid and sides of the car. Other special features include a fiberglass hood with functional air-induction scoops, specially-painted white super stock wheels and wide-oval tires with raised white side lettering."

The release concluded: "Oldsmobile 442's with this specific styling treatment created particularly for the pace car will be seen at Oldsmobile dealerships throughout the country in May."

Of course, many Olds performance fans wanted a pace car replica. The company complied with some 626 replicas; 358 Cutlass S convertibles carrying the standard 350 powerplant and 268 442 models carrying the brutish 455 engine, the same powerplant that powered the real pacer (in an upgraded version).

In 1970, Oldsmobile made the most of the Brickyard duty by launching a large national advertising campaign. The campaign focused on the introduction of the awesome 455 powerplant, and of course, the good Doc made his appearance. **Oldsmobile advertisement**

When the good Doc first put his 455-powered 4-4-2 on the road, he figured he had a pacesetter.

Now it's official!

The motion-minded folks at Indy have just named 4-4-2 the official pace car for this year's classic.

It's easy to see why. Its standard V-8 has a pace-setting 455-cu.-in. displacement. Nobody in its class offers more. Its valve system is revolutionary, featuring positive valve rotators for more efficient performance, longer engine life. Its special suspension with front and rear stabilizers? Fast becoming the most imitated in the business.

Ready to set a pace of your own? See your Olds dealer and test-drive a 4-4-2 or other Olds. You'll find that great performance runs in the family.

OLDS 4-4-2 SPECS

Engine type	H.C. Rocket V-8
Displacement	455 cu. in.
Bhp	365 at 5000 rpm
Torque, lb.-ft.	500 at 3200 rpm
Bore x stroke, in.	4.125 x 4.250
Compression ratio	10.50-to-1
Combustion chamber volume, min. allowable	91.72 cc
Min. cyl. head vol.	69.75 cc
Min. deck clearance	.002 below
Carburetion	Quadrajet 4-bbl
Camshaft duration Intake/exhaust (Sync)	294°/296°
Camshaft overlap Intake/exhaust (Sync)	68°
Total valve lift Intake/exhaust	.472
Valve diameter (Max.) Intake	2.077
Exhaust	1.630
Brakes	9.5" drums
Transmission	Full sync h-d 3-on-the-floor, Hurst Competition Shifter
Axle (Sync)	3.08 ratio
Exhaust system	Full duals
Suspension	FE2
Has h-d springs, shocks, rear control arms, plus stabilizer bars front and rear Wheels	H-d 14" with 7" rim
Tires	G70

bias-belted with white stripe
Strato Bucket Seats . . Std. Lightweight fiberglass hood, functional scoops, big hood stripes, chromed hood tie-downs, and low-restriction air cleaner (W25), available.

Oldsmobile 4-4-2

You've got to believe that the 1970 442 got tons of publicity from the Indy 500. The Olds pace car is shown leading the pack of thirty-three snarling race cars. Pace car replicas are among the most desirable Olds muscle collectibles. **Indianapolis Motor Speedway**

Oldsmobile reaped a ton of publicity when a caravan of 159 replica pacers made its way from Lansing, Michigan, to be turned over to Brickyard track officials.

Forty-nine of the pacers (including the pair that would pace the race) were at the Brickyard for the May festivities. All carried the 365hp 455ci mill, power disc brakes, power steering, and the Rocket Rally Pack which provided such extras as an AM-FM eight-track stereo, W-25 option ram-air hood, tilt wheel, dual-gate Hurst shifter, and numerous gauges.

The actual Y-74 pace car option for 1970 (which required an extra $380) consisted of the Porcelain White paint, Force Air dual-intake fiberglass hood, dual side view mirrors, wide oval tires with raised white lettering, and blacked-out rocker panel moldings.

Most noticeable, though, were the identifying pace car decals which completely covered the door panels. Also, just aft of the main decal was the "500

Oldsmobile flaunted its 1970 Indy pace car honor in a heavy advertising campaign. Here, a post card carries the message. **Oldsmobile literature**

A pair of dashing 1970 Olds pace car replicas decorate the
landscape. The replicas were basically factory 442s with
pace car decorations.

Talk about a rare possession! Don Yeager of Ohio has one of the actual 1972 pace cars, complete with the highly–modified powerplant used to pace at the Brickyard. This car also bears the flags it carried in the race. **Don Yeager**

Festival" emblem. By the way, 1970 Indy race winner Al Unser, Sr. reportedly still has the pacer replica he received for winning the race.

The two pace cars that actually paced the Memorial Day classic were modified for their duties. The fact that the cars had to be "souped up" for the pacing duty was the norm for pace cars during this time period. The first pace car to perform the pacing duties in stock trim appeared in the mid-eighties.

The awesome pair of cars that paced the race carried W-30 heads, a modified Quadrajet carb, an aluminum intake manifold, a recurved W-30 distributor, and a heavy-duty radiator with a clutch fan. The '69 Hurst/Olds donated the tail pipes and mufflers. Since stopping on a dime was of paramount importance, the pacer was also fitted with larger rear brakes. Reportedly, the "real pacers" were able to squat to a stop from about 130mph in just 480 feet.

To meet the demands of pacing, the dynamic duo carried 3.42 rear ends, 0.19 higher than the replica pacers. Finally, the transmissions were altered to

A pair of 455 powerplants were available with the 1972 pace car replicas. Horsepower was listed at 300 and 270.

raise the shift points to 6000rpm. These babies were solid thirteen-second quarter-mile performers.

So, what happened to this super-desirable pair of muscle pacers? Well, number one (the car that paced the race) is still around, reportedly languishing in a garage in Lansing, Michigan. The pacer had gone back to Oldsmobile after the race and was sold to a private party. Pacer number two (used only for warm up laps) is said to have been destroyed when it departed a flatbed truck on which it was being hauled.

1972

The pace car honor was bestowed on the Oldsmobile hood two years later. And for the first of several times, the pacer would be a Hurst/Olds conversion. Since there was already a Hurst/Olds that model year, one that many rate as one of the best-looking muscle cars ever, it was the easy choice for the '72 pace car.

The model looked like a pace car even if you didn't add the appropriate Indy lettering. In fact, with its gold race-style striping, it looked like it should be participating in, rather than pacing, the race.

The Brickyard detailing consisted of the standard lettering on the doors, Indy 500 flags just above the Hurst emblems on the front quarters, and "500 Festival" and a huge Hurst/Olds decal on the rear flanks. Inside, a 1972 Hurst/Olds Indy pace car plaque was mounted on the glove box door.

Hurst built 500 replicas besides the two pacers. Reportedly, there were only 500 sets of pace car decals ordered. Seventy of the pacers (including the two genuine articles) made it to the May festivities. Several of that number (supposedly six) were pacer replica station wagons.

Like the 1972 Hurst/Olds, two Cutlass models, the Supreme Holiday hardtop and the Supreme convertible, were the base models for the pace cars.

Needless to say, it's going to be tough to find one of these vehicles, with only 500 produced. And it's probably not surprising to learn that a number of H/Os have been modified to "create" more pace cars. Unfortunately, there was no vehicle identification number (VIN) differentiation between the H/O and the pace car.

Two versions of the 455 powerplant could be had with the pace car livery, the standard 270nhp engine, and an optional 300nhp W-30 powerplant. This was the final year for an Olds mill to advertise over 300hp, but the Hurst look continued, including another pace car just two years later.

Again, there's the question of what happened to those original pacers. The location of number two is well known; it's the property of Don Yeager.

Talk about owning a rare pace car! Don's genuine 1972 number two pacer is one of the rarest Olds pace cars in private hands.

Yeager explains that Mark Donohue won the 1972 race and was awarded a replica model for that accomplishment. To commemorate that win, Yeager

In 1974, Oldsmobile again was selected to lead the pack at the Indy 500. Even though the muscle era was over, this heavy hauler still looked like it could run with the best. The two available powerplants produced 180 and 250nhp. **Oldsmobile advertisement**

drove the car in the 1992 Indy parade with Donohue's son riding in the car.

He's had the car redone exactly the way it was for that Memorial Day so long ago. It looks like it could still perform those pacing duties, too. The status of the number one pacer is unknown.

1974

If finding a 1970 or 1972 pacer seems impossible, you might want to look for a 1974 model. The two-year trend continued, with Hurst again building the Memorial Day machine in 1974.

Production consisted of the two pacers, about 100 Delta 88 Limited Edition convertibles, several station wagons, and 1,800 Cutlass replica models.

Indianapolis Motor Speedway President Tony Hulman also had a specially-built pace machine manufactured for his own use, a 1974 Cutlass salon with swivel bucket seats.

To meet the 130mph Indy requirement, Hurst made special modifications to the real pacers. The pacers top was removed, effectively creating convert-

A distinctive Indianapolis Motor Speedway decal was positioned atop the air cleaner of the 1974 Olds Indy pace car.

The genuine 1974 Olds pace car in the pits at Indy. Note the "W-30" and "Indianapolis Motor Speedway" decals on the front quarter, pace car decal on the door, and the Hurst identification on the rear quarter. **Indianapolis Motor Speedway**

ibles. In addition, Hurst installed a chrome-moly roll bar (tilted slightly forward) directly over the back seat. The bar was tied to the car's frame and strengthened with steel tubing to restore chassis rigidity lost with the removal of the top.

The suspension was modified with beefy front and rear sway bars, heavy-duty shocks, and extremely stiff springs. The rubber was the new-for-the-time Goodyear GT radials.

Under the hood, there was a custom-built 455 mill. We're talking full-race here with a high-capacity oil pump, heavy-duty cooling system, forged pistons, custom rods, custom cam, a modified four-barrel carb, dual exhaust, and an "old-time" compression ratio of 10.5:1. Although never officially released, the horsepower was well over 300 net horses.

To halt this hauler, the genuine pacers carried power disc/drum brakes with metallic linings. There was also a beefed-up Turbo 400 transmission. Not surprisingly, these machines achieved sub-fourteen-second quarter mile performance at over 100mph.

The replica Cutlass pacers were modified by Hurst and looked much like the real pacers. The Hurst modifications included a special Tierra roof, enlarged and reshaped rear quarter windows, and Goodyear Poly-glass GT belted tires.

The Indy identification was again distinctive with huge "Official Pace Car" lettering along with gold and

This is the official factory photo of the 1977 Olds Indy pace car. The replica versions had the 185nhp 403ci powerplant. Even though horsepower was down from the monstrous ratings of the late sixties and early seventies, 185 wasn't bad for the time period. Indianapolis Motor Speedway

The 1977 pace car models were fitted with a 403ci power-plant which provided a not-too-muscular 185nhp. The car's color scheme consisted of black and grey.

Avid race fan James Garner drove the pace car, a striking red Calais, for the 1985 Indy 500. It was the seventh time an Oldsmobile paced the race. **Oldsmobile**

black accent striping, a unique hood ornament, and the expected Indy pace car decals. The pace car also carried a padded vinyl top with a simulated roll bar, flat-black hood louvers, splash guards, lock lugs for the wheels, and a complete set of gauges.

Two powerplants were offered with the pacer replicas, the Y-77 350ci engine which was rated at 180nhp, and an optional 455ci engine rated at 250nhp. When the latter engine was ordered, a W-30 decal was carried on the front quarters directly below the Indy 500 insignia.

1977

The final Olds pacer of the seventies was based on the Delta 88 Royale, a marginal muscle car at best.

Not since 1960 had a full-sized bodystyle been used for a pace car (the Cutlass was used in 1970, 1972, and 1974).

A stylish paint scheme accented with red stripes and wheels really set off this silver and black pacer. The Indy 500 lettering was carried on the doors while the Indy emblem was on the roof pillar. Finally, large block "Oldsmobile" lettering was on both sides of the hood.

Approximately 2000 replicas were built, with a list price of $6,316. Considering the flashy styling and solid performance of the model, it wasn't a bad price.

The pace car powerplant displaced 403ci and carried a 185nhp, which would equate to over 200bhp. Since the muscle car era was pretty much a memory by this time, the powerplant's economical 18mpg performance was widely touted. Road tests of the pace car recommended the $31 optional handling and suspension package.

Dale Gessaman has one of the rare 1977 pace cars, and he shows it off daily. A used car dealer in

The factory-modified powerplant of the 1985 Indy pacers was a 215hp screamer. The engines were special versions of the 2.7 liter L-4 powerplant. **Oldsmobile**

Dayton, Ohio, Gessaman displays the car in his showroom for all to see. Also displayed with Gessaman's car is a montage of A. J. Foyt cars and parts. He is a big fan of A. J., who won his fourth Indy in 1977 and was awarded a pacer replica for winning that race.

Although the '77 pace car was marginal muscle, the actual pacers were killers, receiving the expected performance modifications to pace the Brickyard. The motors that Oldsmobile built for these cars used the same 403ci, but the modifications pushed the power up to about double the stock output.

The powerplant featured ported and polished heads, big-block valves, W-30 valve springs, a W-31 cam, and TRW forged pistons. It was one tough mill; too bad it didn't make it to the street. But the times just weren't right for that kind of muscle.

1985

Muscle was coming back in the mid-eighties, and Oldsmobile was ready with its first pace car in eight years. For the first time, the Olds pacer would do its thing without a V-8.

The actual pace car used a special 2.7 literL-4 en-

gine, derived from the standard Calais powerplant provided about 215hp at 6500rpm. An electronic control module controlled the base air-fuel mix, acceleration fuel enrichment, and power enrichment by monitoring a number of functions including throttle position and rpm.

Power was pumped through an extensively modified three-speed automatic transmission. To handle the more-than-doubled horsepower output, a special engine mounting system was fabricated. To maximize the power to the ground, this dashing pacer used gas-filled shocks and revised spring rates. Complementing the suspension were special sixteen-inch wheels and low-profile tires.

Second best to the pacer were the numerous replicas that were built. The so-called Calais 500 carried the red and platinum metallic color scheme of the real pacers. The replicas also featured a "Calais 500" emblem on the hood, the "Indy 500" emblem on the sail panel, and the "Official Indianapolis 500

Performance was making a comeback at Oldsmobile in the late eighties, and the 1988 Indy pace car exemplified that trend. A specially–designed turbocharged 2.3 liter mill pumped out an impressive 250hp. The powerplant was a version of the famous Olds Quad 4. **Oldsmobile**

For the second time in the eighties, the Oldsmobile rocket emblem took the stage at Indianapolis. With a modified Quad 4 under the sleek hood, this Cutlass Supreme was definitely up to its pacing duties. Note the Indy logo on the rear quarter.

Pace Car" on the doors.

Inside, modified reclining buckets with silver leather inserts with Carmine vinyl trim, Indy 500 floor mats, and other Indy logos made this machine stand out.

Although the muscle wasn't up to previous standards (with 2.5 and 3.0 liter powerplants available), the 1985 model sure *looked* muscular and for many, that was what it was all about.

1988

The 1988 pace car signaled Oldsmobile's return to performance. The '88 pacer featured power and dazzling looks. A specially-built Quad 4 turbocharged powerplant pumped an impressive 250nhp out of only 2.3 liters.

The engine's compression ratio was 8.8:1 and turbo boost was set at 7.5lb-ft. The engine was fuel injected and turbocharged with an air-to-air intercooler. It maintained its stock bore and stroke, and was fitted with forged pistons and crankshaft. The remainder of the powertrain included a three-speed turbo Hydra-Matic transaxle with a 3.33:1 final drive.

The Cutlass Supreme was selected for the Indy honor, and was modified by Cars and Concepts, a well-known custom body shop. The pacer incorporated a deeper front air dam and a dashing black finish that was accentuated by racy silver trim. The Indy lettering appeared in the same silver, accented in red.

Production was low, with Cars and Concepts constructing 50 street-legal convertibles while Oldsmobile made 200 coupes in pace car trim.

The interiors featured specially-upholstered front and rear bucket seats, plus three-point competition seatbelts for both driver and passenger. On the actual pacers, there was a Halon fire extinguisher system, a fuel cell, and removable roll bar.

The five pace cars and convertible replicas were the first production cars to have the fighter-type Head-Up Display (HUD) designed by Hughes and Delco. This technology projected the instrument display onto the windshield, in the driver's direct line of sight.

Chapter 6

Other Olds Muscle Cars

All the famous members of the Oldsmobile muscle family have been discussed; the 442, the W Machines, the Hurst/Olds, and so on. Throw in the colorful Indy pacers, and that about does it for those golden years. Right? Well, almost. There are several more that deserve mention.

Rallye 350 (1970)

The first in the semi-muscle category is the Rallye 350, which was produced only in 1970. By the standards of the time, the 350ci, 310bhp machine wasn't considered real muscular. But race car looks and horsepower exceeding 300 make it easy to call the Rallye 350 a muscle car.

Oldsmobile had an ulterior motive for designing the Rallye 350: it was called "insurance." Younger drivers just couldn't afford the premiums for performance cars with a weight-to-power ratio of less than ten. This 3,500 pound, 310hp machine didn't quite make the "expensive" category as far as the insurance industry was concerned.

The Rallye 350 was available on the F-85 Sports Coupe, the Cutlass, and the Holiday version of the Cutlass S. Oldsmobile advertised the car as a dynamite-looking attention-grabber. "It's an all new action look. From the wheels up, from the price down...It's the boldest scene steeler that ever toured main street," as one ad put it. The Rallye 350 was hard to resist. So, what distinguished it from the competition?

Right off the bat, there was its dramatic Sebring Yellow color scheme and color-matched urethane-coated bumpers. The yellow bird was beautifully detailed with side and rear sport stripes, blacked-out

The 1968 Cutlass was an attractive machine with 310 ponies available under the hood. A car like this could provide a reasonably-priced muscle restoration project.

hood, black-patched hood splotches, Rallye 350 rear quarter decals, and D-36 Sport Mirrors. Finally, there was a rakish W-35 rear spoiler and N-66 slotted Super Stock II wheels.

The rear bumper looked like it had been done in a rod shop with the taillights set into the bumpers and notched at the bottom to integrate the N-10 dual-exhaust megaphones. The optional FE-2 Rally Suspension package brought handling on a par with the model's appearance. The package included stiffer

The replacement for the W-31, the Rallye 350's 350ci L-74 mill put significant punch under the hood. The model sported the functional W-25 fiberglass hood and a Rochester four-barrel carb. Horsepower was rated at a none-too-shabby 310.

The Rallye 350 was a real looker, with bright yellow paint and dazzling detailing. The one-year model had power under the hood to accompany the flashy sheet metal. The identification was carried on the rear quarter in bold block letters.

springs, heavy-duty control arms, and front and rear sway bars.

Although performance wasn't the strong suit of this looker, it was enough to attract 3,547 buyers. The production breakdown included 1,020 F-85s, 2,367 Cutlass S hardtop coupes, and a mere 160 Sports Coupes.

The 350ci L-74 mill perked at 10.25:1 compression ratio carrying log-type exhaust manifolds, cast-iron intake, and Rochester Quadrajet four-barrel carburetor. Breathing was enhanced by ram-air scoops on the W-25 fiberglass hood which enabled cold air injection at full throttle. An impressive 390lb-ft dose of torque at only 3200rpm complemented the mill's 310hp at 4800rpm.

If you wanted a little more performance, Olds offered a special kit with lighter retainers that could provide an extra 200rpm of redline.

Transmission choices were plentiful; three- and four-speed manuals and the M-38 Turbo 350 auto-

Left
The fabulous-looking Rallye 350. The 350ci mill was worth 310hp and 390lb-ft of torque.

The SX model was introduced in 1970 as a personal luxury car. Equipped with the right options, the machine could become quite muscular. Oldsmobile History Center

The bold yellow paint of the Rallye 350 contrasted with the model's sedate interior. You might expect the Rallye name to appear on the glove box door, but that didn't happen with this yellow bird.

You had to look closely to determine if a 1971 model carried the SX option. The letters were outlined in a small rectangle below the Cutlass scripting.

In its final year of production, the SX option typically accompanied the Y-79 package, which included the L-32 powerplant, a 455ci engine equipped with a four-barrel carburetor. The 1971 SX wasn't a big seller, with only 2,117 going out the dealers' doors.

The base model for the first 442, the 1964 F-85, was a solid performer on its own.

Even the Cutlass packed plenty of performance under the hood. As many as 310 horses were available from this Cutlass S 350 mill.

Although the Cutlass never fell into the classic performance category, it still had a stylish, louvered hood. This one graces a 1968 model.

No air induction scoops on the 1968 Cutlass, but its gutsy 350 powerplant and dynamite looks make it a marginal muscle car.

According to muscle enthusiasts, this impressive-looking standard Cutlass was pretty much ignored in the performance camp. Pity!

matic were offered. The standard gear ratio was 3.23:1, but 3.42 and 3.91 gears could be ordered. The Rallye 350 was a low fifteen-second performer in the quarter.

Considering the Rallye 350's mid–year release (February 18, 1970, to be exact), the car didn't do that badly. Unfortunately, it wouldn't be around the following year. With new emission controls and the downturn in muscle interest, Olds didn't take a chance on another "Yellow Submarine."

Charles Baxter owns one of the best Rallye 350s in the country, but he didn't find it that way.

"I bought the car off a wrecker when it was on its way to the car crusher," Baxter explained. "Even after I got the car, it was in such bad condition that I considered parting it out. Then I realized what a rare car this one-year special was, and decided that it was sure worth the effort to restore it."

Baxter says that with its 310hp, it is not classi-

fied as a muscle car, "but it's sure one in my mind."

Cutlass SX (1970–1971)

Some models in the Olds arena didn't start off being muscle cars, but ended up in that category. The two-year SX (Code-79) was such a car. The SX could become quite muscular with a little innovative ordering. Buyers who chose their options wisely drove off the showroom with a legitimate muscle car.

The SX started out as a personal luxury car available in a formal roofline coupe and convertible. The small SX tag and modest appearance of the car didn't do justice to the luxurious interior. The driver was treated to simulated wood vinyl, rough-grained upholstery, and chromed plastic beading just to name a few.

The SX powertrain featured the L-33 455 mill

Cutlass S in the late sixties spelled big-time looks and performance, with a 310hp rating from the top 350ci powerplant.

pumping out an impressive 320hp. Those numbers are especially impressive considering the engine breathed through a two-barrel carb! The $139 SX option also included dual exhaust and a 442–style rear bumper with exhaust pipe cutouts.

Economy was one of the advantages of this luxurious cruiser. With the standard Turbo 400 automatic and high rear-end gearing (2.78), the SX practically sipped gasoline compared to its four-barrel 455–powered brothers. If you liked the looks of the SX, but weren't particularly enthralled with the "family style" powertrain, you could go a little nuts and have the factory build your own SX muscle car.

First, you could order the high-compression W-32 455 mill rated at 365hp. Suddenly, you had a rocket! You could also order the W-25 Force Air hood, Rallye Sport Suspension, and lower rear-end gearing. It might have said SX on the sheet metal, but this specially-ordered machine was a muscle car in every sense of the word.

The only year both the SX and the W-32 were available was 1970. Both were available as options on the Cutlass Supreme. Reportedly, there were 7,197 SX-optioned Cutlass S models built that-year.

In the final year of the SX (1971) a confusing

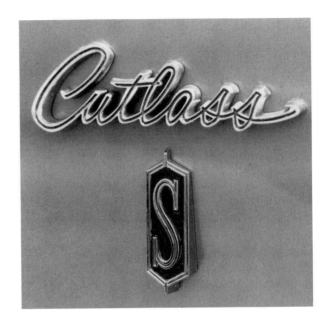

Although you never hear of the Cutlass S being mentioned in muscle car conversation, you'd better not say that in front of the Kentucky owner of this beautiful machine.

Here's looking at you! The attractive grill design of the 1968 Cutlass blended well with the model's racy design.

The 350ci engine was capable of 310hp at 4800rpm, the compression ratio was an impressive 10.25:1, and the carburetor was a Rochester 4GC. Although this engine didn't get the attention of the 442 and W models, it's performance was worthy of note.

change occurred. With the downturn of performance, it would seem that the L-33 two-barrel 455 was a perfect match for the times. But that wasn't the case, as the powerplant was dropped in favor of the L-32 four-barrel carb version of the 455.

The SX package (again the Y-79 option) for year two was still available (again only with the Cutlass Supreme), with the package requiring an extra $151. Customer interest tumbled, however, to only 2,117.

SX package components for 1971 were similar to the previous year, with the rear cutout bumper and M-40 Turbo Hydra-matic transmission. The front-quarter SX emblems were also in place for the final year of this interesting muscle mutation. Although certainly not of the same caliber as its more famous W and Hurst machines, locating and restoring one of these milder 455–powered machines could make for an interesting, and certainly rare, muscle car.

These classy stripes made the 1969 Cutlass resemble the muscle machines of the era. Considering the 350ci, 310hp engine under the hood, the Cutlass might deserve muscle machine recognition.

The SX letters appeared again in the following years on other models, one example being the 1980 Omega. Olds called it the Y-66 option, and it was strictly an appearance package. For $303, you got a blacked-out lower body, special wheel covers, and a classy-looking rear spoiler. Unfortunately, the horses under the hood didn't even approach the SX ratings of a decade earlier.

Just Plain Cutlass Muscle

With all the famous Olds muscle of the late sixties to early seventies, it is often forgotten that it was possible to put well over three hundred horses under the hood of the base Cutlass.

The 1967 Delmont model could be ordered with a 330ci/320hp or a 425ci/365hp powerplant.

The redesigned 1971 Cutlass was an excellent seller with a V-8 under the hood. Over 34,000 of the model were sold.

The 1971 Cutlass Supreme hood featured a full-length groove which continued down the vertical grill.

F-85 and Cutlass standard powerplant displacements increased 20ci (to 350) for 1968 and were rated at 310hp.

In 1969, it was possible to order the 350, 400, and 455 powerplants with standard F-85 and Cutlass models. Even without a W-30 or 442 badge on your flanks, you could still mount a significant challenge at the stop light.

Similar offerings were available for the Cutlass models in 1970. The 350 mill that could be ordered with the Cutlass S produced 310bhp and provided an impressive 310lb-ft of torque. A manual three-speed was standard with this punchy powerplant. But compression ratios dropped like a rock in 1971,

All brake and backup lights were contained within the rear bumper while the exhaust bugles fit into the lower portion of the bumper.

Horsepower was low on the regular Cutlass line in 1972. The standard 350 mill, the biggest engine available for the model, was rated at 180bhp.

and with it went this engine's performance.

The company still flirted with performance during the seventies, even though sometimes it was in looks only. You could still get a 455 (downgraded) with the Cutlass in 1972. The 1973 and 1974 Cutlass models could also be acquired with 180hp, 350ci powerplants, but after that, the venerable mill was dropped.

The 455 was available through the mid-seventies, but it was available only on the lead sled 88 and 98 models, where the power was needed to push the two-and-one-half-ton monsters. These machines couldn't be called muscle cars simply because of their big engines.

Final Note

During the Oldsmobile muscle era, an assortment of model configurations can be classified as muscle cars, says Oldsmobile Club of America official Ed Shaudys. "Olds dealer and sales persons could order just about any setup the buyer desired. Thus, while there was a basic norm, we do find many interesting muscle variations which were not advertised," Shaudys explains.

He continues: "During this era, it was possible to order special engines and drivetrain combinations. For example, a 400ci engine could be ordered for a Cutlass as a special order...I even know of a '67 Vista Cruiser (station wagon) ordered with a 400. I also know of a '70 442 ordered without the high-performance powertrain, but with the other 442 components. Certainly, these kind of variations challenge judges at meets, but they were all done to satisfy customer demands, and of course, to sell that car."

The 4.0 liter V-8 for the 1995 Aurora model brings V-8 performance to the nineties. The 250hp killer features an aluminum upper block, five four-bolt main bearings, aluminum heads, and four overhead camshafts. **Oldsmobile**

Chapter 7

Modern Olds Muscle

While a majority of Oldsmobile performance fans think of the sixties and seventies as the muscle years, the company has been quietly rebuilding a performance image in the late eighties and early nineties with a number of high-performance powerplants.

Although it wasn't a big-block screamer, the 2.3 liter Quad 4 powerplant, introduced with the 1987 Cutlass Calais, was a step back toward performance. Featuring dual chain-driven overhead camshafts and four valves for each of the four cylinders (that's right, only four cylinders), the mini-screamer offered efficiency, power, fuel economy, and easy maintenance.

Available in all trim levels of the Calais, the Quad 4 was the exclusive powerplant in the impressive new Cutlass Calais International Series. The 1994 version of the Quad 4, the LG0 version, provided an impressive 170hp at 6200rpm with 150lb-ft of torque at 5200rpm. The powerplant came standard with a five-speed manual transmission, and was available only with the Achieva SC and SL models.

In the nineties, a number of impressive V-6 powerplants pumped out horsepower in ever-increasing numbers. The 135hp 4.3 liter Vortec with central port fuel injection (available with the Bravada model) was capable of 200hp at 4500rpm and 260lb-ft of torque at only 3600rpm.

The L-27 3800cc V-6 produced 170hp at 4800-rpm and was available with a number of different models. With 225lb-ft of torque, the gutsy V-6 was available with a four-speed automatic transmission.

Up to 185hpwas available from the 3100cc SFI L-82 V-6 equipped with sequential fuel injection. Finally, there was the LQ1 3400cc double-overhead cam V-6, with a pounding 210 horses. Who said performance wasn't in vogue for the nineties?

Still, there wasn't a V-8 to be found, at least that was the case until 1995, when the new Aurora powerplant was introduced. The sixties were back!

The revolutionary thirty-two-valve powerplant has a displacement of four liters and 250hp. But it's the way that those ponies are made that is interesting.

First, there's a die-cast aluminum upper block with integral cast-iron cylinder bores, and a lower block that combines five four-bolt main-bearing caps in an aluminum casting to enhance rigidity and provide an oil distribution function. The aluminum cylinder heads are equipped with pentroof combustion chambers, four valves per cylinder, and centrally–located spark plugs.

Muscle arrived in a four-cylinder powerplant. The sixteen-valve Quad 4 dohc engine first saw light in 1987 and offered a combination of power and low maintenance. **Oldsmobile**

*The Aerotech, an experimental performance prototype, used
a right-side-mounted, highly-modified Quad 4 powerplant.*
Oldsmobile drawing

The 1988 Cutlass Calais was the first to feature the new 2.3 liter Quad 4 engine. It marked Oldsmobile's return to performance. Oldsmobile

Four overhead camshafts are driven by three roller chains that require neither maintenance nor periodic replacement. The pistons are aluminum with full-floating wrist pins. The die-cast aluminum oil pump is equipped with a windage tray, baffles, and an optical oil level sensor.

There is a direct ignition system with four coils, dual-tipped platinum spark plugs, and no moving parts or distributor. The coolant system carries an inlet thermostat to minimize temperature and pressure cycling.

Thirty-two-valve technology is really nothing new to Oldsmobile engineers. They built and tested a thirty-two-valve dohc powerplant in 1967. An aluminum

The famous "W" was back with the 1991 Quad 4 W-41 mill. Although the horsepower wasn't of the caliber of earlier V-8 big-block days, this high-revving powerhouse provided exciting performance with less than half the displacement. Oldsmobile

The W-41 powerplant was around again in 1992, and continued to be a popular choice among buyers.

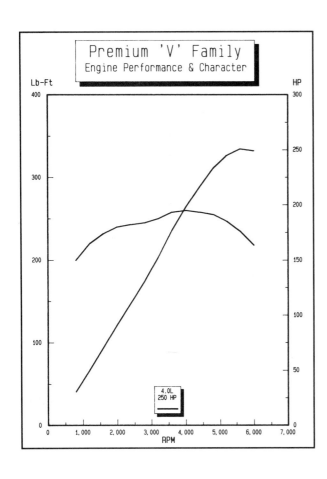

Premium 'V' Family
Engine Performance & Character

4.0L
250 HP

Maximum horsepower from the Premium V Aurora power-plant is achieved at about 5500rpm, maximum torque of 240lb-ft at about 4000rpm. Oldsmobile chart

twin-turbo V-8 was also developed for Can-Am racing in the late sixties, and it produced an amazing 650hp.

The powerplant and 4T80-E transaxle are controlled by Aurora's powertrain control module for coordinated operation in every conceivable driving circumstance. The 4T80-E has four forward speeds, fourth being an overdrive gear. In addition, the model features a lock-up torque converter and two driver-selectable modes: normal and performance. In the performance mode, downshifts are calibrated to maximize the Aurora's responsiveness.

Oldsmobile performance is back, and one can but imagine where it will go in the next century.

The 1994 Cutlass Supreme convertible also demonstrated big horsepower numbers with its LQI 3400cc double-over-head-cam V-6 that provided 210hp at 5200rpm and 215lb-ft of torque at only 4000rpm. **Oldsmobile**

Left
Big horsepower numbers were available in 1994 from the 98 Regency Elite. The L-27 3.8 liter was worth 170hp at 4800rpm, while the L-27 supercharged 3800cc V-6 was worth an impressive 225hp at only 200 additional rpm. **Oldsmobile**

Index